Holiday Treats

A Cookbook
with Pizzaz

By Barbara C. Jones
and
Sheryn R. Jones

BCJ Publications
1901 South Shore Drive
Bonham, Texas 75418
903-583-2832

Dedicated to a Loving
Husband and Father

Cover Design by
Karen Halbrook

cookbook
resources

541 Doubletree Drive
Highland Village TX 75067
(972) 317-0245

INTRODUCTION

"Holiday Tastes" is a cookbook that makes the holidays fun — even for the cook. Enjoy your traditional recipes, but give your dining table a new look for a few days of the holidays. We have new and different breakfast breads and muffins; we have special salads that brighten your table and your palate; we have spreads and dips to tempt and tease; we have desserts to treat and eat — with gusto and bravado!

Christmas is not only a time to celebrate the birth of the Christ Child, it is a time to gather with family and good friends. Each one of us like to please our loved ones with gifts and fabulous foods. We give you the means to plan a beautiful and boutiful table — we show you how to carve the turkey, how to trim the ham, how to make good use of your leftovers. We have many recipes that will definitely give your "sweet tooth" a workout! We give you many delicious food gifts to make — look for the "package" on certain recipes.

"Holiday Tastes" is your map to find just the right recipes to please your family and friends. For an afternoon reception, you can't beat our Very Special Coffee Punch. For an informal get-together, we have delightful "finger foods" like Hanky Panky Bites, Smoked Salmon Log, Oat Munchies, Almond Squares Spectacular or Macadamia Candy. We have traditional foods like turkey and dressing, Cranapple Wiggle and Christmas Lemon Pound Cake "to die for". Then we have Hidden Secret Muffins, Praline French Toast and Christmas Preserves that will start your day with vigor and vitality. Then there's nibble foods like Reindeer's Rapture, Cherry Pecan Slices or Spiced Pecans. Cakes, pies, cookies and candies are a must at Christmas time and we would like to give you the inspiration to be the aristocratic queen of your kitchen!

Happy Holiday, Barbara and Sheryn Jones

TABLE OF CONTENTS

Beverages

VERY SPECIAL COFFEE PUNCH

I Promise — This Will Make a Hit!

1 (2 ounce) jar instant coffee
2 quarts hot water
2 1/4 cups sugar
2 quarts half and half
1 quart ginger ale
1 pint heavy cream, whipped
1/2 gallon French vanilla ice cream

Dissolve instant coffee in hot water. Cool; add sugar and half and half, mixing well. Chill. When ready to serve, pour coffee-sugar mixture in punch bowl, add chilled ginger ale, whipped cream and ice cream. Let some chunks of ice cream remain. This will make 60 four ounce servings.

Everyone will be back for seconds!

CHRISTMAS PARTY PUNCH

3 cups sugar
2 1/2 quarts water
1 (6 ounce) package lemon gelatin
1 (3 ounce) can frozen orange juice concentrate, thawed
1/3 cup lemon juice
1 (46 ounce) can pineapple juice
3 tablespoons almond extract
2 quarts ginger ale, chilled

Combine sugar and 1 quart water. Heat until sugar is dissolved. Add gelatin, stirring until dissolved. Add fruit juices, remaining 1 1/2 quarts water and almond extract. Refrigerate. When ready to serve, place in punch bowl and add chilled ginger ale. This will make 50 servings.

The almond extract really gives this punch a special taste!

Ruby Christmas Punch

2 (6 ounce) cans frozen orange juice concentrate
4 cups water
2 (46 ounce) cans red Hawaiian punch
1 (46 ounce) can pineapple juice
1 (48 ounce) bottle cranapple juice
2 liters ginger ale, chilled

In two gallon bottles, combine orange juice, water, Hawaiian punch, pineapple juice and cranapple juice; stir well. Chill. Place in punch bowl. Just before serving, add ginger ale. Makes 2 gallons.

*The cranapple juice in this punch
really makes it a "Christmas" special!*

Green Party Punch

1 (3 ounce) package lime gelatin
1 cup boiling water
1 (6 ounce) can frozen limeade
1 (6 ounce) can frozen lemonade
1 quart orange juice
1 quart pineapple juice
1 tablespoon almond extract
2 to 3 drops green food coloring
1 liter ginger ale, chilled

Dissolve lime gelatin and boiling water; stirring well. In a gallon bottle, combine dissolved gelatin, limeade, lemonade, orange juice, pineapple juice, almond extract and food coloring. Chill. When ready to serve, add the ginger ale. Serves 32.

*This punch would also be a good one to use
when the party is close to St. Patrick's Day!*

Simple and Easy Punch — But Very Good

Just chill bottles of Welch's Sparkling White Grape Juice. What could be easier than that!

RECEPTION PUNCH

4 cups sugar
6 cups water
5 ripe bananas, mashed
Juice of 2 lemons
1 (46 ounce) can pineapple juice
1 (6 ounce) can frozen undiluted orange juice
2 quarts ginger ale

Boil sugar and water for 3 minutes. Cool. Blend bananas with lemon juice. Add pineapple and orange juice. Combine all ingredients except the ginger ale. Freeze in a large container. To serve, thaw 1 1/2 hours; then add ginger ale. Punch will by slushy. Serves 40.

SPARKLING CRANBERRY PUNCH ✓

Ice mold for punch bowl
Red food coloring (optional)
2 quarts cranberry juice cocktail
1 (6 ounce) can frozen lemonade, thawed
1 quart ginger ale, chilled

Pour water in a mold for the ice ring; add red fool coloring to make the mold brighter and prettier. Mix cranberry juice and lemonade in pitcher. Refrigerate until ready to serve. When serving, pour cranberry mixture into punch bowl and add the ginger ale. stirring well. Add decorative ice mold to the punch bowl. Serves 24 cups.

STRAWBERRY SPRITZER

1 (10 ounce) package frozen strawberries in syrup, thawed
1 (24 ounce) bottle white grape juice, chilled
1 (12 ounce) can club soda, chilled

Process strawberries and syrup in a blender until smooth, stopping once to scrape down sides. Stir together strawberry puree and white grape juice; add club soda. Yields 7 cups.

CHAMPAGNE PUNCH

1 bottle Rose wine
1 cup honey
2 (6 ounce) cans frozen orange juice, undiluted
3 liters champagne

Chill all ingredients and mix together. Pour into a beautiful punch bowl.

This makes a good "wedding reception" punch, too!

KAHLUA

3 cups hot water
1 cup instant coffee granules
4 cups sugar
1 quart vodka
1 vanilla bean, split

In a large saucepan combine hot water and coffee; mixing well. Add sugar and bring to a boil. Boil 2 minutes. Turn off heat and cool. Add vodka and vanilla bean. Pour into a bottle or jar and let set for 30 days before serving. Shake occasionally.

If you happen to have some of the Mexican vanilla, you can make "instant" Kahlua by using 3 tablespoons of Mexican vanilla instead of the vanilla bean. Then you do not have to wait 30 days.

AMARETTO

3 cups sugar
2 1/4 cups water
1 pint vodka
3 tablespoons almond extract
1 tablespoon vanilla (not the imitation)

Combine sugar and water in a large pan. Bring mixture to a boil. Reduce heat. Let simmer 5 minutes, stirring occasionally. Remove from stove. Add vodka, almond and vanilla. Stir to mix well. Store in airtight jars.

Appetizers

DIPPER'S DELIGHT

1 (8 ounce) package cream cheese, softened
2 tablespoons milk
1 (2.5 ounce) package smoked, sliced, pressed pastrami, cut into
    very fine pieces
3 green onions, finely sliced (tops too)
3 tablespoons finely chopped green pepper
1/4 teaspoon black pepper
1/3 cup mayonnaise
1/2 cup chopped pecans
1/2 teaspoon Tabasco
1/4 teaspoon garlic powder
1/4 teaspoon seasoned salt
1/2 teaspoon Italian herbs

In mixer bowl, whip together the cream cheese and the milk until creamy. Add remaining ingredients and mix well. Refrigerate. Serve with crackers.

This is so good you'll want to make it into a sandwich!

HOLIDAY CRABMEAT SPREAD

1 (8 ounce) package cream cheese, softened
1 (3 ounce) package cream cheese, softened
1 bunch green onions, finely chopped (tops too)
1 teaspoon lemon juice
3/4 teaspoon seasoned salt
1/2 teaspoon Worcestershire
1 tablespoon dried parsley flakes
2 (6 1/2 ounce) cans crabmeat, drained and flaked
1 cup cocktail sauce
1/2 cup chopped pecans

In mixing bowl, combine cream cheese, onion, lemon juice, seasoned salt, Worcestershire and parsley flakes. Beat until fluffy. Spread on the bottom of a 9 inch glass pie plate or similar pretty serving platter. Flake the crabmeat and distribute evenly over the cream cheese. Spoon cocktail sauce over crabmeat and then sprinkle with pecans. Chill until ready to serve. Serve with crackers.

Hanky Panky Bites

1 pound sausage
1 pound lean ground beef
1 pound mild Mexican Velveeta cheese, cubed
1 teaspoon garlic powder
1 teaspoon oregano
1/2 teaspoon seasoned salt
1 tablespoon Worcestershire
Loaf of white sandwich (square) bread
Paprika
1 (6 ounce) bottle green stuffed olives

Brown meats, stirring until crumbly. Drain. Stir cheese into meat, stirring and cooking over low heat until cheese melts. Add seasonings; mix well and remove from heat. Trim crusts from bread and cut each slice into fourths. Spread about a tablespoon of the meat mixture on bread squares and place on cookie sheets. Sprinkle paprika on squares. Place 1/2 of an olive (cut side up) in the middle of each square. Punch olive down firmly into the meat so it won't come off. Freeze. After they are frozen, take off cookie sheet and place in baggies for the freezer. Then when you're ready to serve, take as many as you want and bake at 350 degrees for 12 to 15 minutes.

Cocky Broccoli Cheese Dip

1 (10 ounce) package frozen chopped broccoli, thawed and drained
2 tablespoons margarine
2 stalks celery, chopped
1 small onion, finely chopped
1 (1 pound) box mild Mexican Velveeta cheese, cubed

Make sure the broccoli is thoroughly thawed and drained (if you will place broccoli between several paper towels and squeeze, it will help get the water out). Place margarine in a large saucepan and saute the broccoli, celery and onion at medium heat for about 5 minutes, stirring several times. Add cheese and heat just until cheese is melted. Serve hot. Serve with chips.

SPINACH CRAB BALLS

1 tablespoon margarine
1 onion, minced
2 (10 ounce) packages frozen chopped spinach, thawed, well
    drained and patted dry
4 eggs
2 tablespoons flour
4 slices bacon, cooked and crumbled
1 stick margarine, softened
1 (7 1/2 ounce) can crabmeat, drained and flaked
2 cups seasoned stuffing, crumbled
1/4 teaspoon pepper
1/2 teaspoon salt
1/2 teaspoon dillweed
1/4 teaspoon garlic powder

Melt margarine in skillet. Stir in onion and saute. Mix thoroughly with
remaining ingredients. Form into 1 1/2 inch balls and place on baking
sheet. Bake at 325 degrees for 15 minutes. Serve warm. (If you want to
make ahead and bake when you're ready to serve — just freeze spinach
balls on the baking sheet; then remove to a baggie to store frozen.)
These can be served plain or with sweet and hot mustard. (see page 87)

SPINACH AND CHEESE SQUARES

1/2 stick margarine
1 cup flour
3 eggs
1 cup milk
1 teaspoon salt
1 teaspoon baking powder
1 teaspoon dry mustard
2 (10 ounce) packages frozen spinach, thawed, drained and
    squeezed dry
8 ounces mozzarella cheese, shredded
8 ounces Cheddar cheese, shredded

Melt margarine in a 9x13 inch baking dish in the oven. In large mixing
bowl, combine flour, eggs, milk, salt, baking powder and mustard. Mix
well. Add spinach and cheeses, pour into pan. Bake at 350 degrees for
30 minutes. When set, cut into squares and serve warm Can be
reheated.

GREAT GRAPE MEATBALLS

1 1/2 pounds lean ground beef
3 eggs
1 teaspoon dried parsley flakes
1/2 teaspoon garlic powder
1 teaspoon seasoned salt
1/2 teaspoon black pepper
1/2 teaspoon dried cilantro leaves
5 slices bread, crumbled in food processor
1 (16 ounce) jar grape jam (not jelly)
1 (12 ounce) jar chili sauce

Combine beef, eggs, parsley, garlic powder, seasoned salt, pepper, cilantro leaves and bread crumbs. Roll into 3/4 inch meatballs. Brown in skillet. Combine jam and chili sauce in a large crock pot or large saucepan. Heat, then add the meatballs to crock pot and simmer for 1 hour. Serve hot, in chafing dish or you can leave in the crock pot if the party is not real formal.

TINSEL TENDERLOIN

1 1/2 pounds whole pork tenderloin
1/4 cup dry white wine
1 teaspoon marjoram leaves
1 teaspoon dried rosemary leaves
1/4 teaspoon garlic powder
1/4 teaspoon black pepper
1/2 teaspoon salt
1/2 stick margarine, melted

Place tenderloin in baking pan. Combine wine, marjoram, rosemary, garlic powder, black pepper and salt; blend well and pour over meat. Cover and marinate at room temperature for 20 minutes. Remove pork from marinade and place on baking sheet. Add margarine to marinade. Preheat oven to 450 degrees. Roast on middle rack of oven for 30 minutes, basting meat thoroughly every 10 minutes. If the meat has not browned a little, turn broiler on just until meat is slightly browned. Remove from oven and allow to cool to room temperature. Slice meat very thin to serve. You can serve the thin slices of the roast on slices of party rye bread if you like.

Smoked Salmon Log

1 (15 ounce) can red salmon
1 (8 ounce) package cream cheese, softened
1 tablespoon lemon juice
2 tablespoons grated onion
1/4 teaspoon salt
1/4 teaspoon liquid smoke
6 tablespoons very finely crushed crackers
1 cup very finely chopped pecans
3 tablespoons minced fresh parsley

Drain salmon; remove skin and bones; flake salmon with fork. In mixer bowl, beat together the cream cheese and lemon juice. Add onion, salt, liquid smoke, crackers and salmon. (Add another spoonful of cracker crumbs if your mixture seems too sticky). Chill several hours or overnight. Spread out a piece of waxed paper and put a very light coat of flour on it. Make a roll with the salmon mixture. Then roll in the pecans and parsley mixture. Roll onto another piece of waxed paper to be able to lift the roll. Chill several hours and serve with crackers.

This is so good, you'll make it all year long!

Sweet and Sour Sausage Balls

1 pound hot pork sausage
1 pound mild pork sausage
2 eggs
1/2 teaspoon seasoned salt
2 cups soft bread crumbs
Sauce:
1 (12 ounce) bottle cocktail sauce
3/4 cup brown sugar
1/2 cup wine vinegar
1/2 cup soy sauce

Mix sausage, eggs, seasoned salt and bread crumbs. Form into small balls. Brown sausage balls and drain. Combine all sauce ingredients and pour over sausage balls. Simmer uncovered for about 1 hour. You could also use a crock pot to simmer the sausage balls — and then, just serve in the crock pot (if it is a real informal occasion).

WONDER DIP

1/3 cup finely chopped green onions
1/2 cup <u>very finely</u> cut broccoli (tiny florets)
1 (8 ounce) can water chestnuts, drained and coarsely chopped
3/4 cup mayonnaise
3/4 cup sour cream
1 (2.7 ounce) jar crystallized ginger, finely chopped
1/2 cup finely chopped pecans
1/2 teaspoon salt
2 tablespoons soy sauce

Mix all ingredients together. Prepare a day ahead and chill. Serve with wheat crackers.

This is really "different" — unique to the palate!

CRAB AND ARTICHOKE SPREAD

1 1/2 cups fresh Parmesan cheese
1 (14 ounce) can artichoke, drained and chopped
1 1/2 cups mayonnaise
1/2 cup finely minced onion
1/2 teaspoon Worcestershire
1/4 cup fine bread crumbs
1/8 teaspoon garlic powder
2 drops Tabasco (optional)
1 (6 ounce) can crabmeat, drained and flaked
Paprika

Mix together the Parmesan cheese, artichokes, mayonnaise, onion, Worcestershire, bread crumbs, garlic powder, Tabasco and crabmeat. Spread onto a buttered 9 inch glass pie plate. Sprinkle a good amount of paprika over the spread. Bake at 350 degrees for 20 minutes. Serve with crackers.

GREEN EYES

4 large dill pickles
4 slices boiled ham
Light cream cheese
Black pepper
Garlic powder

Dry off pickles. Lightly coat one side of the slices of ham with the cream cheese and sprinkle a little pepper and a little garlic powder on each slice. Roll the pickle up in the slice of ham coated with the cream cheese mixture. Chill. Cut into circles.

SEAFOOD SPREAD

1 (8 ounce) package cream cheese, softened
1/3 cup mayonnaise
1/3 cup sour cream
3 hard-boiled eggs, mashed
1 (8 ounce) can crabmeat, drained and flaked
2 (8 ounce) cans tiny shrimp, drained and chopped
1/4 onion, very finely chopped
1 stalk celery, very finely chopped
1 teaspoon Creole seasoning
Several dashes Tabasco

Combine cream cheese, mayonnaise, sour cream and boiled eggs in mixer bowl. Beat until fairly smooth. Add crabmeat, shrimp, onion, celery, Creole seasoning and Tabasco; mix well. Serve with crackers. This can also be used as a dip or to make good sandwiches.

SPICY PARTY SPREAD

1 cup chopped pecans
1 tablespoon margarine, melted
2 (8 ounce) packages cream cheese, softened
1 package Taco seasoning
2/3 cup shredded Cheddar cheese
1 cup picante sauce
1 bunch green onions, chopped (tops too)

Bake pecans in a shallow pan with the margarine at 275 degrees for about 25 minutes. In mixer bowl, beat together the cream cheese, taco seasoning and Cheddar cheese. Stir in picante sauce, pecans and onions. Spoon into a greased 9 inch glass pie plate. Bake, covered in a preheated oven at 325 degrees for 15 minutes. Spread on Wheatsworth crackers.

ELEGANT CRAB DIP

1 (6 1/2 ounce) can white crabmeat, drained
1 (8 ounce) package cream cheese
1 stick butter (the real thing)

In a saucepan, combine crabmeat, cream cheese and butter. Heat and mix thoroughly. Transfer to hot chafing dish. Serve with chips.

DEVILED EGG SPREAD

3 hard-boiled eggs, mashed
1 (3 ounce) package cream cheese, softened
4 ounces Monterey Jack cheese, grated
1/2 cup mayonnaise
1/2 teaspoon prepared mustard
1/4 teaspoon salt
1/2 teaspoon white pepper
3/4 cup finely grated chopped pecans
1 (4 ounce) can chopped green chilies

In mixing bowl, combine eggs, cream cheese, Jack cheese, mayonnaise, mustard, salt and pepper, beat well. Add chopped pecans and green chilies; mix. Refrigerate.

A fun way to use this spread is to quarter small green bell peppers and fill with Deviled Egg Spread.

HOT ARTICHOKE SPREAD

1 (14 ounce) can artichoke hearts, drained and chopped
1 (4 ounce) can chopped green chilies
1 cup mayonnaise
1 cup grated mozzarella cheese
1/4 teaspoon white pepper
1/2 teaspoon garlic salt
Paprika

Remove any spikes or tough leaves from artichoke hearts. Combine all ingredients and mix well. Place in Pam sprayed 9 inch baking dish and sprinkle paprika over top. Bake at 300 degrees for 30 minutes. Serve warm with tortilla chips or crackers.

Southwestern Dip

2 (8 ounce) packages cream cheese, softened
1/4 cup lime juice
1 tablespoon cumin
1 teaspoon salt
1 teaspoon cayenne pepper
1 (8 ounce) can whole kernel corn, drained
1 cup chopped walnuts
1 (4 ounce) can chopped green chilies
3 green onions, chopped (tops too)

In mixing bowl, whip cream cheese until fluffy; beat in lime juice, cumin, salt and cayenne pepper. Stir in corn, walnuts, green chilies and onions. Refrigerate. Serve with tortilla chips.

*Who would ever expect to put corn and walnuts in a dip —
try it, it's great!*

Party Sausages

1 cup catsup
1 cup plum jelly
1 tablespoon lemon juice
2 tablespoons prepared mustard
2 (5 ounce) packages tiny smoked sausages

In a saucepan, combine all ingredients except sausages; heat and mix well. Add sausages and simmer for 10 minutes. Serve with cocktail toothpicks.

Asparagus Rolls

20 thin slices white bread
1 (8 ounce) package cream cheese, softened
3 tablespoons margarine, softened
1 egg
1/2 teaspoon seasoned salt
20 canned asparagus spears, drained
1 1/2 sticks margarine, melted

Remove crusts from bread and flatten slices with a rolling pin. In mixer bowl combine cream cheese, margarine, egg and seasoned salt. Spread mixture evenly over bread slices. Place an asparagus spear on each one and roll up. Dip in melted margarine to coat all sides. Place on cookie sheet and freeze until ready to bake. Preheat oven to 400 degrees. Cut frozen rolls into thirds and bake for 15 minutes or until lightly browned. Serve immediately.

HORSEY SHRIMP DIP

1 (8 ounce) package cream cheese, softened
2/3 cup mayonnaise
1 tablespoon lemon juice
3 tablespoons creamy horseradish
1/4 cup chili sauce
1/2 teaspoon Creole seasoning
1/4 teaspoon garlic powder
2 (8 ounce) cans shrimp, drained
2 green onions, chopped (tops too)

In mixing bowl, combine cream cheese, mayonnaise, lemon juice, horseradish, chili sauce, Creole seasoning and garlic powder; blend well. Chop shrimp and onions. Add to cream cheese mixture and blend. Refrigerate. Serve with chips.

SASSY ONION DIP

1 (8 ounce) package cream cheese, softened
1 (8 ounce) carton sour cream
1/2 cup chili sauce
1 package dry onion soup mix

In mixer bowl, beat cheese until fluffy. Add remaining ingredients and mix well. Cover and chill. Serve with strips of raw zucchini, celery, carrots or turnips.

FLORENTINE DIP

1 (10 ounce) package frozen, chopped spinach, thawed
1 (8 ounce) package cream cheese, softened
2/3 cup mayonnaise
2 hard-boiled eggs, finely chopped
1/4 teaspoon pepper
3/4 teaspoon seasoned salt

Drain spinach by using several sheets of paper towels and blot spinach very dry. In a mixing bowl, combine cream cheese, mayonnaise, eggs, pepper and seasoned salt; beat. Add spinach and mix. Refrigerate. Serve with vegetable dippers.

Breads & Brunch

APRICOT BREAD EXTRAORDINAIRE

3 cups flour
1 1/2 teaspoons baking soda
1/2 teaspoon salt
2 cups sugar
1 1/2 cups oil
4 eggs
1 teaspoon vanilla
1 (5 ounce) can evaporated milk
1 1/4 cups apricot butter
1 1/4 cups chopped pecans
Apricot Butter:
1 1/4 cups finely chopped apricots, soaked overnight in water
1 cup sugar

Mix together flour, baking soda and salt. Add sugar, oil, eggs vanilla and evaporated milk. Mix thoroughly. Add apricot butter and pecans; blend. Pour into 2 greased and floured loaf pans and bake at 350 degrees for 1 hour and 5 to 10 minutes or until loaf tests done.

To make apricot butter, soak apricots overnight in water to cover. Add sugar and simmer 10 minutes or until soft. Cool completely before adding to recipe.

This is "it" for apricot lovers!

GLAZED LEMON BREAD

1/2 cup shortening
1 cup sugar
2 eggs
1 1/2 cups flour
1 teaspoon baking powder
Pinch of salt
1/2 cup milk
1 1/2 teaspoons lemon extract
Rind of 2 lemons, grated
1/2 cup chopped pecans
Glaze:
Juice of 2 lemons
1/4 cup sugar

Cream shortening and sugar, add eggs and beat thoroughly. Sift together flour, baking powder and salt. Add alternately with milk to creamed mixture. Add lemon extract and grated lemon rind. Fold in chopped pecans. Pour into a greased and floured loaf pan and bake at 325 degrees for 60 to 65 minutes. Test with toothpick. For glaze, combine lemon juice and sugar in a saucepan and bring to a boil. Pour over hot bread while still in pan. Use toothpick to pierce bread so glaze will run into loaf.

MINCEMEAT BREAD

1 3/4 cups flour
1 1/4 cups sugar
2 1/2 teaspoons baking powder
1/2 teaspoon salt
2 eggs, beaten
1 teaspoon vanilla
1 1/2 cups prepared mincemeat
3/4 cups pecans
1/3 cup shortening, melted
Glaze:
1 cup powdered sugar
1 tablespoon milk
1/4 cup finely chopped pecans

In a large bowl combine flour, sugar, baking powder and salt. In medium bowl combine eggs, vanilla, mincemeat and pecans. Mix well. Stir in the melted shortening; mixing quickly. Pour egg mixture into dry ingredients. Stir only enough to moisten flour. Spoon batter into a greased and floured loaf pan. Bake at 350 degrees for 1 hour or until toothpick inserted in center comes out clean. Cool 15 minutes and remove from pan. Cool completely. Mix powdered sugar and milk and stir until smooth. Stir in pecans. Spread over the top of loaf. Slice bread and spread a little margarine on each slice and toast.

Wonderful!

BUTTERNUT BREAD

1 butternut squash
2 1/2 cups flour
2 teaspoons baking powder
1 teaspoon baking soda
1 teaspoon cinnamon
1/2 teaspoon ground allspice
1/2 teaspoon ground ginger
1/2 teaspoon ground nutmeg
1/2 teaspoon salt
1 1/2 sticks margarine, softened
1 cup granulated sugar
1/2 cup packed brown sugar
2 eggs
1 (8 ounce) carton sour cream
1 teaspoon vanilla
1 cup chopped pecans

Trim ends off the squash and halve it lengthwise. Scoop out and discard the seeds. Cut the squash into 2 inch pieces, leaving the skin on. Steam squash until completely tender, about 25 minutes; drain well. When squash is cool enough to handle, use spoon to scoop flesh away from skin. Mash squash with a fork. Set aside. Sift flour, baking powder, baking soda, spices and salt together in bowl; set aside. In mixer bowl cream the margarine and both sugars until smooth. Add eggs; beat well. Add sour cream, vanilla and 1 cup of the butternut squash (discard remaining); mix well. Stir in the dry ingredients just until combined. Stir in pecans. Pour into a greased and floured loaf pan. Bake at 350 degrees for 1 hour and 10 to 15 minutes or until a toothpick comes out clean. Cool in pan 15 minutes. Then turn out on rack and continue cooling.

This bread is a little more trouble, but well worth it. It's different and delicious; very good toasted for breakfast.

JINGLE BREAD

3/4 cup raisins
1 pound hot sausage (raw)
1 1/2 cups light brown sugar
1 1/2 cups sugar
2 eggs
1 cup chopped pecans
3 cups flour
1 teaspoon ginger
1 teaspoon allspice
1 teaspoon cinnamon
1 teaspoon baking powder
1 teaspoon baking soda
1 cup cold coffee

In a saucepan cover raisins with water and simmer for 5 minutes; drain. Combine sausage, sugars and eggs. Stir in pecans and raisins. Combine flour, spices and baking powder in separate bowl. Stir soda into coffee. Blend coffee and flour mixture into sausage mixture. (This is when you can have fun mixing with your hands.) Pour into 2 greased and floured loaf pans. Bake at 350 degrees for 1 hour and 10 minutes or until bread tests done. Refrigerate.

Yes the sausage is right in the bread! A slice or two, warmed or toasted, makes a great breakfast!

STRAWBERRY BREAD

3 cups flour
1 teaspoon soda
1 teaspoon cinnamon
1/2 teaspoon salt
2 cups sugar
2 (10 ounce) cartons frozen strawberries, thawed
1 1/4 cups oil
4 eggs, beaten
1 teaspoon red food coloring

Combine flour, soda, cinnamon, salt and sugar in mixer bowl. With your spoon, make a "well" in the dry ingredients and add strawberries, oil and eggs. Mix well. Add food coloring, mixing well. Pour into a greased and floured loaf pan. Bake one hour at 350 degrees.

Great for finger food at parties or as sandwiches with cream cheese and pecans. Red is "in"!

BLUEBERRY LEMON BREAD

1 3/4 cups flour
1 teaspoon baking powder
1/4 teaspoon salt
3/4 stick (6 tbs) margarine, softened
1 cup sugar
2 eggs
2 teaspoons grated lemon peel
1/2 cup milk
1 1/2 cups frozen blueberries, thawed and well drained
1/2 cup sugar
3 tablespoons lemon juice

Combine flour, baking powder and salt in a small bowl; set aside. In a mixing bowl, using electric mixer, cream margarine with sugar until mixture is light and fluffy. Add eggs one at a time, beating well after each addition. Add lemon peel and mix in dry ingredients alternately with milk, beginning and ending with dry ingredients. Fold in blueberries. Spoon batter into a greased and floured loaf pan. Bake 1 hour and 5 minutes or until toothpick comes out clean. During last 15 minutes of baking time, bring the 1./2 cup sugar and 3 tablespoons lemon juice to a boil in a small saucepan, stirring until sugar dissolves. When loaf is done and still hot, pierce top several times with a toothpick. Pour hot lemon mixture over loaf while still in pan. Cool 30 minutes in pan on a rack. Turn bread out of pan and cool completely on rack.

Wonderful toasted for breakfast!

APPLESAUCE PECAN BREAD

1 cup sugar
1 cup applesauce
1/3 cup oil
2 eggs
2 tablespoons milk
1 teaspoon almond extract
2 cups flour
1 teaspoon soda
1/2 teaspoon baking powder
3/4 teaspoon cinnamon
1/4 teaspoon salt
1/4 teaspoon ground nutmeg
3/4 cup chopped pecans
Topping:
1/2 cup chopped pecans
1/2 teaspoon cinnamon
1/2 cup packed brown sugar

Combine sugar, applesauce, oil, eggs, milk and almond extract. Mix well. Combine all dry ingredients and add to sugar mixture; mix well. Fold in pecans. Pour into greased and floured loaf pan.

For topping, combine pecans, cinnamon and brown sugar. Sprinkle over batter. Bake at 350 degrees for 1 hour and 5 minutes. Test for doneness. Cool on rack.

CARAMEL ROLLS

9 tablespoons margarine, softened (divided)
1 cup light brown sugar
1/4 cup water
1/2 cup chopped pecans
2 (8 ounce) cans refrigerated crescent dinner rolls
1/4 cup sugar
2 teaspoons cinnamon

In ungreased 9x13 inch pan, melt 5 tablespoons margarine in oven. Stir in brown sugar, water and pecans. Set aside. Separate each can of roll dough into 4 rectangles. Pinch perforations together to seal. Spread with 4 tablespoons softened margarine. Combine sugar and cinnamon; sprinkle over dough. Starting at shorter side, roll up each rectangle. Cut each roll into 4 slices, making 32 pieces. Place in prepared pan. Bake at 375 degrees for 20 to 25 minutes, until golden brown. Invert immediately to remove from pan. Serve warm.

HIDDEN SECRET MUFFINS

Filling:
1 (8 ounce) package cream cheese, softened
1 egg
1/3 cup sugar
1 tablespoon grated orange rind
Muffin:
2 sticks margarine, softened
1 3/4 cups sugar
3 eggs
3 cups flour
2 teaspoons baking powder
1 cup milk
1 teaspoon almond extract
1 cup chopped, toasted almonds (page 86)

Beat cream cheese, eggs, sugar and orange rind together; set aside. Cream margarine and sugar until light and fluffy. Add eggs one at a time, beating after each addition. Stir flour and baking powder together. Add flour and milk alternately to margarine and sugar mixture, beginning and ending with flour. Add almond extract and fold in almonds. Fill 26 lightly greased muffin tin half full muffin batter. Spoon about 1 heaping tablespoon of filling in each muffin tin. Top filling with muffin batter. Bake muffins at 375 degrees for 20 to 25 minutes or until muffin just bounces back when pressed and until they are lightly browned.

These are what my Daddy would have called "Larripin good"!

APPLESAUCE SPICE MUFFINS

2 sticks margarine, softened
1 cup brown sugar
1 cup granulated sugar
2 eggs
1 3/4 cups applesauce
2 teaspoons cinnamon
1 teaspoon allspice
1/2 teaspoon ground cloves
1/2 teaspoon salt
2 teaspoons baking soda
3 1/2 cups flour
1 1/2 cups chopped pecans

Cream together the margarine and sugars. Add eggs, applesauce, spices, salt, baking soda and flour. Mix well. Add pecans; stir will. Pour into 28 greased muffin tins or pans with paper liners. Bake at 375 degrees for 16 minutes.

Apricot Pineapple Muffins

1/3 cup very finely cut up dried apricots
1 stick margarine, softened
1 cup sugar
1 egg
1 (8 ounce) can crushed pineapple, undrained
1 1/4 cups flour
1/2 teaspoon baking soda
1/2 teaspoon salt
1 cup quick rolled oats

Cut apricots up with your kitchen scissors. Set aside. With mixer, cream margarine and sugar together. Add egg and pineapple; beat well. Add all dry ingredients; mixing well. Fold in apricots. Spoon into well greased muffin tins (or use the paper liners) and bake at 350 degrees for 20 minutes. Makes 12 muffins.

This is a winner!

Pimento Cheese Biscuits

2 cups flour
3 teaspoons baking powder
2 tablespoons sugar
1 teaspoon salt
A scant 1/8 teaspoon cayenne pepper
1 1/2 cups shredded sharp Cheddar cheese
1/2 stick margarine
4 tablespoons shortening
1 (2 ounce) jar chopped pimento, drained
1/4 cup finely chopped green bell pepper
1/2 cup plus 2 tablespoons milk

Combine flour, baking powder, sugar, salt and cayenne pepper. Add cheese and mix well. Cut margarine and shortening into flour mixture with pastry blender (or fork) until consistency of coarse cornmeal. Add pimento and green pepper. Make a well in the dry ingredients and add milk. Using a fork, stir to combine until mixture forms a ball. (You may need a little extra milk if it seems too dry to roll out.) Turn dough onto a floured surface and roll out to a 1/2 inch thickness and cut into 2 inch rounds. Bake biscuits on an ungreased cookie sheet at 400 degrees for 12 to 15 minutes.

EAGLE YEAST BREAD

8 cups sifted flour (divided)
1 tablespoon sugar
1 tablespoon salt
2 yeast cakes
1 can Eagle Brand condensed milk
1/3 cup oil

Combine 6 cups flour, sugar and salt. Set aside. Soften yeast in small amount of warm water. Add Eagle Brand condensed milk, oil and enough warm water to measure 4 cups. Mix well. Add to flour mixture. Mix well. Add remaining 2 cups flour, mixing well. Knead 10 minutes. Place in greased bowl, turning to greased surface. Let rise, covered for 1 1/2 to 2 hours or until doubled in size. Divide into 3 portions. Place in 3 greased loaf pans. Let rise 40 minutes. Bake at 350 degrees approximately 40 minutes. Brush with melted butter.

BUTTERMILK ROLLS

2 yeast cakes
1/4 cup warm water
1 1/2 cups lukewarm buttermilk
3 tablespoons sugar
1/4 cup oil
4 1/2 cups flour
1/2 teaspoon soda
1 teaspoon salt

Soak yeast in warm water. Add warm buttermilk, sugar and oil. Sift into this mixture the flour, soda and salt. Form into dough and knead 10 minutes. Shape into rolls and place in 2 greased pie pans. Let rise 30 to 45 minutes. Bake at 400 degrees for 15 to 20 minutes. Brush with melted butter. Yields 1 1/2 to 2 dozen rolls.

CRUNCHY BREAD STICKS

1 package hot dog buns
2 sticks margarine, melted
Garlic powder
Paprika
Parmesan cheese

Take each half bun and slice in half lengthwise. Using a pastry brush, butter all bread sticks and sprinkle a light amount of garlic powder and just a few sprinkles of paprika and Parmesan cheese. Place on cookie sheet and bake at 225 degrees for about 45 minutes.

You won't believe how good these are!

MINCEMEAT CRUMB COFFEE CAKE

Topping:
2 tablespoons flour
1/3 cup sugar
1 1/2 teaspoons cinnamon
2 tablespoons margarine
Cake:
1 1/2 cups flour
3/4 cup sugar

2 teaspoons baking powder
1/2 teaspoon salt
1 egg
1/2 cup milk
3 tablespoons margarine,
    melted and cooled
1 cup prepared mincemeat
1/2 cup chopped pecans

Grease and flour a 10 inch deep dish pie plate. For topping, stir together dry ingredients and then cut in margarine until mixture becomes crumbly. Set aside.

In mixer bowl, stir together flour, sugar, baking powder and salt. Beat egg with milk and melted margarine. Add egg mixture to flour mixture, stirring until mixture is smooth. Stir in mincemeat and pecans. Spread batter into prepared pan and sprinkle with topping. Bake at 375 degrees for about 40 minutes or until tester comes out clean. Serve warm.

GOOD MORNING COFFEE CAKE

2 1/3 cups flour
1 1/2 cups sugar
3/4 teaspoon salt
3/4 cup shortening
2 teaspoons baking powder
3/4 cup milk
2 eggs
1 teaspoon vanilla
1 (3 ounce) package cream cheese, softened
1 can Eagle Brand condensed milk
1/3 cup lemon juice
1 can peach pie filling, cut each peach slice into 3 chunks
2 teaspoons cinnamon
3/4 cup chopped pecans

In a mixing bowl, combine flour, sugar and salt; cut in shortening until crumbly. Reserve 1 cup crumb mixture. To remaining crumb mixture, add baking powder, milk, eggs and vanilla. Beat on medium speed for 2 minutes. Spread into a greased and floured 9x13 inch baking dish. Bake at 350 degrees for 25 minutes. In another bowl, beat cream cheese and condensed milk until fluffy; gradually fold in lemon juice, peach pie filling and cinnamon. Spoon this mixture over hot cake. With the remaining crumb mixture., add pecans and sprinkle on top of cake. Bake another 25 minutes. Let set 10 minutes before serving. Serve warm.

BREAKFAST BAKE

1 pound hot sausage, cooked and crumbled
2 tablespoons dried onion flakes
1 cup grated Cheddar cheese
1 cup Bisquick
1/4 teaspoon salt
1/4 teaspoon pepper
4 eggs
2 cups milk

Preheat oven to 350 degrees. Place cooked and crumbled sausage in a Pam sprayed 9x13 inch glass baking dish. Sprinkle with onion flakes and cheese. In mixing bowl, combine Bisquick, salt, pepper and eggs. Beat well. Add milk and stir until fairly smooth. Pour over sausage mixture. Bake for 35 minutes. If you want to make one day and cook the next morning, just keep refrigerated before cooking. To cook the next morning, add an extra 5 minutes to the cooking time since you would be taking it right out of the refrigerator. Serves 8.

For a brunch, add 1 (8 ounce) can
of whole kernel corn, drained.

QUESADILLA PIE

1 (4 ounce) can chopped green chilies
1/2 pound sausage, cooked
2 cups grated Cheddar cheese
3 eggs, well beaten
1 1/2 cups milk
3/4 cup biscuit mix
Hot salsa

Spray a 9 inch pie pan with Pam. Sprinkle the green chilies in pie pan; then the cooked sausage and Cheddar cheese. In a separate bowl, mix together the eggs, milk and biscuit mix. Pour over the chilies, sausage and cheese. Bake in a preheated 350 degree oven for 30 minutes. Serve with salsa on top of each slice. Serves 6.

HOMEMADE EGG SUBSTITUTE

6 egg whites
1/4 cup instant nonfat dry milk powder
2 teaspoons water
2 teaspoons oil
1/4 teaspoon ground turmeric

Combine all ingredients in electric blender and process 30 seconds. Refrigerate. 1/4 cup is the equivalent to one egg.

Quick Christmas Breakfast

1 (8 ounce) package crescent dinner rolls
1 pound hot pork sausage, cooked and drained
5 egg, beaten
3/4 cup milk
1/2 teaspoon salt
1/4 teaspoon black pepper
1 (8 ounce) package shredded mozzarella cheese

Line a 9x13 inch baking dish with crescent rolls, pressing seams together. Cover with sausage. In a medium bowl, combine remaining ingredients and pour over sausage. Bake at 350 degrees for 30 minutes. Let stand 5 minutes before serving.

This can be frozen before baking; then place in refrigerator the night before serving and bake the next morning. Add 5 minutes to baking time because you would be taking it right out of refrigerator.

Rise and Shine Eggs

2 cups finely chopped ham
1 cup shredded Monterey Jack cheese
1/2 cup shredded Cheddar cheese
1 tablespoon flour
8 eggs
1 cup milk
Salsa

Grease a 9x13 inch glass baking dish. Sprinkle ham evenly over bottom, followed by cheeses. Sprinkle flour over cheeses. With the back of a large spoon, slightly hollow 8 places for eggs (away from the edge of glass). Break the eggs into the indentations and lightly break yolks with tip of knife. Pour milk on top and bake for about 30 minutes (depending on preference for soft or hard-boiled eggs). Serve with salsa on the side.

SAUSAGE APPLE RING

2 pounds bulk sausage
1 1/2 cups crushed cracker crumbs
2 eggs, slightly beaten
1/2 cup milk
1/4 cup minced onion
1 cup finely chopped apple
Scrambled eggs

Preheat oven to 350 degrees. Thoroughly combine sausage, cracker crumbs, eggs, milk, onion and apple. Press lightly into greased ring mold, then turn out into a shallow baking pan or sheet cake pan. Bake for 50 minutes. (This may be baked partially for 30 minutes, then drain off fat, refrigerate and finish baking when ready to serve.) Drain well before placing on a serving platter. Fill center with scrambled eggs and serve immediately. It would take about a dozen eggs to fill the center.

PRALINE FRENCH TOAST

8 large eggs, beaten
1 1/2 cups half and half
4 tablespoons brown sugar
1/4 teaspoon salt
2 teaspoons vanilla
8 thick slices French bread (or the thick square bread)
1 stick margarine
3/4 cup brown sugar, firmly packed
2/3 cup maple syrup
1 cup chopped pecans

In a small bowl, combine eggs, half and half, brown sugar, salt and vanilla. Pour half into a 9x13 inch pan. Cover with bread slices, then top with remaining egg mixture. Cover and refrigerate overnight. Before serving, preheat oven to 350 degrees. In another 9x13 inch glass baking dish, melt margarine and stir in brown sugar, maple syrup and pecans. Cover margarine mixture with soaked bread slices and bake 30 to 35 minutes until puffed and brown. If not slightly browned, turn on broiler for a minute or two. Cut into squares and serve plates. Serve immediately. Serves 8.

Salads

CHRISTMAS SALAD

1 (6 ounce) package lime gelatin
1 (8 ounce) can crushed pineapple, drained
Juice from pineapple plus water to make 1 cup
1 (8 ounce) package cream cheese, softened
1 cup miniature marshmallows
1 (8 ounce) carton Cool Whip
1 (6 ounce) package raspberry gelatin
1 cup boiling water
1 (12 ounce) package frozen raspberries, thawed
1 (8 ounce) can crushed pineapple, undrained

Dissolve lime gelatin in a large mixing bowl with 1 cup of boiling pineapple juice and water. Add cream cheese and beat on slow speed of mixer. Fold in marshmallows and pineapple. Cool in refrigerator about 30 minutes and fold in Cool Whip. Pour into Pam sprayed 9x13 inch glass dish and refrigerate until set. In separate bowl, dissolve raspberry gelatin with the boiling water. Add raspberries and crushed pineapple; pour over first layer of gelatin mixture. Refrigerate until firm.

SPICY CRANBERRY SALAD

1 (6 ounce) package raspberry gelatin
1/4 teaspoon salt
1/2 teaspoon cinnamon
1/8 teaspoon cloves
1 cup boiling water
2 cans whole cranberry sauce
1 (8 ounce) can crushed pineapple, undrained
1 can mandarin oranges, drained

Place gelatin, salt, cinnamon and cloves in a large mixing bowl and pour boiling water over gelatin. Mix until gelatin is well dissolved. Add both cans cranberry sauce, pineapple and oranges. Pour into a Pam sprayed 9x13 inch dish and refrigerate until firm.

Cranberries are a must for Christmas!

APRICOT SALAD

1 (6 ounce) package apricot gelatin
3/4 cup boiling water
1 (8 ounce) package cream cheese, softened
2 tablespoons sugar
3/4 cup chopped pecans
1 (8 ounce) can crushed pineapple, undrained
1 (16 ounce) can apricots, drained
1 (8 ounce) carton Cool Whip

In mixer bowl, mix gelatin with boiling water until gelatin is dissolved. Add cream cheese and beat until fairly smooth. Stir in sugar, pecans and pineapple. Cut each apricot half into fourths. Fold apricots and Cool Whip into gelatin mixture. Pour into a 9x13 inch glass dish. Refrigerate.

Apricots are an every day treat!

YULETIDE SALAD

1 (6 ounce) package red raspberry gelatin
1 cup boiling water
1 can cherry pie filling
1 (8 ounce) can crushed pineapple, undrained
3/4 cup chopped pecans
1 (6 ounce) package lime gelatin
3/4 cup boiling water
1 (8 ounce) package cream cheese, softened
1 (8 ounce) can crushed pineapple, undrained
3/4 (8 ounce) carton Cool Whip
4 or 5 drops green food coloring

Dissolve raspberry gelatin in boiling water. Add cherry pie filling, pineapple and pecans. Pour into a Pam sprayed 9x13 inch glass dish. Chill until partially set. In mixer bowl, dissolve lime gelatin in 3/4 cup boiling water. Mix well. Add cream cheese and whip (slowly at first) until cream cheese has melted. Add the pineapple and cool in refrigerator. When green mixture begins to thicken, fold in Cool Whip and green food coloring. Spread on top of the raspberry mixture and refrigerate.

Red and green are special for Christmas.

CRANBERRY WIGGLE

1 (6 ounce) package cherry gelatin
1 1/2 cups boiling water
1 (16 ounce) can whole cranberry sauce
1 (15 ounce) can crushed pineapple, undrained
1 cup chopped apples
1 cup chopped pecans

Dissolve gelatin in boiling water; mixing well. Add cranberry sauce, pineapple, apples and pecans. Pour into a Pam sprayed 9x13 inch glass dish and refrigerate. Stir about the time it begins to set so the apples won't all stay on top. Serves 12.

A tradition for a family friend.

CINNAMON SALAD

3 cups water
2 (6 ounce) packages cherry gelatin
2/3 cup cinnamon red hot candies
1 (25 ounce) jar applesauce
2 teaspoons lemon juice
Filling:
2 (8 ounce) packages cream cheese, softened
1 cup mayonnaise
1 cup chopped walnuts

In a large saucepan, heat water to boiling; add gelatin and stir until dissolved. Lower heat to moderately low and add candies. Continue heating and stirring until candies are dissolved. Remove from heat; add applesauce and lemon juice. Pour half of gelatin mixture into a 9x13 inch baking dish. Set aside remaining gelatin mixture at room temperature. Place first layer in freezer for about an hour or until set. In a mixer bowl, combine cream cheese and mayonnaise until fairly smooth. Mix in walnuts. When first layer of gelatin is firmly set, spread cream cheese mixture over top. Chill about 30 minutes; then pour remaining gelatin mixture over top. Refrigerate several hours. Serves 15.

PINK POINSETTIA SALAD

1 (6 ounce) package raspberry gelatin
1 cup boiling water
1 can blueberry pie filling
1 (8 ounce) can crushed pineapple, undrained
1 cup chopped pecans
1 (8 ounce) carton Cool Whip

Dissolve gelatin in boiling water, stirring well. Stir in pie filling, crushed pineapple and pecans. Set in refrigerator for about 30 minutes to cool. When chilled, fold in Cool Whip. Pour into a Pam sprayed 9x13 inch glass dish. When ready to serve, cut in squares and serve on a lettuce leaf. This makes a very pretty salad for a luncheon. Serves 12.

Pretty plus delicious!

LIME MINT SALAD

2 (16 ounce) cans crushed pineapple, drained
1 (6 ounce) package lime Jello
1 (10 ounce) package tiny marshmallows
1 (12 ounce) carton Cool Whip
1 teaspoon pineapple extract
1/2 teaspoon mint extract
1 (8 ounce) box buttermints, crushed

Mix pineapple, dry Jello and marshmallows in bowl and let set overnight at room temperature. Next day fold in Cool Whip, pineapple extract, mint extract and buttermints. Pour into a 9x13 Pyrex dish and freeze. Set out of freezer a few minutes before cutting and serving. Serves 12.

The buttermints make this recipe a special treat.

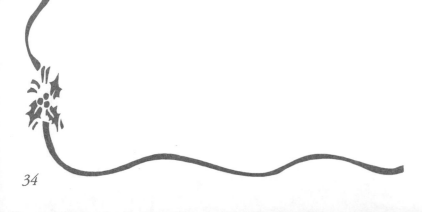

INCREDIBLE STRAWBERRY SALAD

2 (8 ounce) packages cream cheese, softened
2 tablespoons mayonnaise
1/2 cup powdered sugar
1 (16 ounce) package frozen strawberries, thawed
1 cup small marshmallows
1 (8 ounce) can crushed pineapple, drained
1 (8 ounce) carton Cool Whip
1 cup chopped pecans

In a large mixing bowl, combine cream cheese, mayonnaise and powdered sugar. Beat until creamy. Fold in strawberries (if strawberries are large, cut them in half), marshmallows, pineapple, Cool Whip and pecans. Pour into a 9x13 inch glass dish. Freeze. Take out of freezer about 15 minutes before cutting and serving. Serves 12.

It really is incredible!

CHAMPAGNE SALAD

3/4 cup powdered sugar
1 (8 ounce) package cream cheese, softened
1 1/2 cups maraschino cherries, cut in half, well drained
1 (20 ounce) can crushed pineapple, drained
2 bananas, mashed
1 (8 ounce) carton Cool Whip
1 cup chopped pecans
1 1/2 cups miniature marshmallows

Cream together sugar and cream cheese. Fold in cherries, pineapple, bananas, Cool Whip, pecans and marshmallows; mix well. Pour into a Pam sprayed 9x13 inch pan and freeze. Thaw 15 minutes before trying to cut in squares to serve.

This is a great "make ahead" salad!

Frozen Holiday Salad

2 (3 ounce) packages cream cheese, softened
3 tablespoons mayonnaise
1/4 cup sugar
1 (16 ounce) can whole cranberry sauce
1 (8 ounce) can crushed pineapple, drained
1 cup chopped pecans
1 cup tiny marshmallows
1 (8 ounce) carton Cool Whip

Cream cheese, mayonnaise and sugar. Add fruit, pecans and marshmallows. Fold in Cool Whip and pour into a greased 9x13 inch shallow Pyrex dish and freeze. When ready to serve, take salad out of freezer a few minutes before cutting into squares.

Creamy Gazpacho Salad

1 can tomato soup
1 envelope plain gelatin
1/4 cup cold water
1 (8 ounce) package cream cheese, softened
1/2 cup chopped celery
1/2 cup chopped bell pepper
1 tablespoon finely chopped onion
1 teaspoon lemon juice
1/2 cup chopped pecans
1 cup mayonnaise
1/3 cup sliced green olives

Heat soup, gelatin and water; blend. Add cream cheese and stir constantly while leaving on medium heat. Blend well. Cool and add remaining ingredients. Pour mixture into a mold or a 9x9 inch Pyrex dish and let set overnight. Cut into squares to serve. Serves 8. To make a main dish, add 1 cup cooked shrimp.

This is a great salad that is not sweet!

A great discovery!

CRANBERRY-CHICKEN SALAD

Layer 1:
1 1/2 envelopes unflavored gelatin
1/4 cup cold water
1 (16 ounce) can whole cranberry sauce
1 (8 ounce) can crushed pineapple
1/4 cup sugar
1 cup chopped pecans
Red food coloring (optional)
Layer 2:
1 1/2 envelopes unflavored gelatin
1/4 cup cold water
1/2 cup water
1 (3 ounce) package cream cheese
3 tablespoons lemon juice
3/4 teaspoon salt
2 cups diced cooked chicken
3/4 cup chopped celery
1/4 cup sweet relish
1 cup chopped pecans

Layer 1: Soften gelatin in cold water. Place cranberry sauce, pineapple and sugar in sauce pan. Heat to boiling point. Add gelatin mixture and stir well. Mix in pecans and red food coloring. Pour into a Pam sprayed 9x13 inch glass dish and chill.

Layer 2: Soften gelatin in 1/4 cup cold water. Place 1/2 cup water, cream cheese, lemon juice and salt in sauce pan. Bring to a boil and stir until cream cheese is dissolved. Stir in gelatin mixture. Fold in chicken, celery, relish and pecans. Pour on top of cranberry mixture. Chill. To serve, cut into squares and put cranberry side up on a bed of lettuce.

CASHEW SALAD

1 (6 ounce) package lemon gelatin
1 cup boiling water
1 quart vanilla ice cream
1 (15 ounce) can fruit cocktail, drained
1 1/4 cups cashew nuts

Dissolve gelatin in boiling water and add ice cream. Stir until melted. Add fruit cocktail and cashew nuts. Blend well. Pour into an 8x11 inch glass dish. Refrigerate overnight.

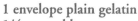

ARTICHOKE SALAD

1 envelope plain gelatin
1/4 cup cold water
1/2 cup boiling water
1 cup mayonnaise (not salad dressing)
1 (14 ounce) can hearts of artichoke, well drained
1/2 (10 ounce) package frozen green peas, thawed, uncooked
2 tablespoons lemon juice
1 (4 ounce) jar chopped pimentos
1 bunch green onions, finely chopped (tops too)
1 1/2 cups shredded mozzarella cheese
1 teaspoon Italian herb seasoning
1/8 teaspoon cayenne pepper
Paprika

Soften gelatin in cold water. Add boiling water and mix well. Add mayonnaise and stir until smooth. Remove any spikes or tough leaves from artichoke hearts and chop. Add all remaining ingredients except paprika. Pour into a ring mold and refrigerate. When ready to serve, slip knife around edges to loosen from mold. Unmold onto a serving plate lined with lettuce. Sprinkle paprika over salad. You could put radishes, olives or black olives, etc., in center of mold when serving.

BROCCOLI NOODLE SALAD

1 cup almonds, toasted
1 cup toasted sunflower seeds
2 packages chicken Ramen noodles (uncooked)
1 package broccoli slaw
Dressing:
3/4 cup oil
1/2 cup white vinegar
1/2 cup sugar

You can toast the almonds and sunflower seeds by toasting them in the oven at 275 degrees for about 15 minutes. Break up Ramen noodles; mix with slaw, almonds, and sunflower seeds. In a separate bowl, mix dressing ingredients. Pour over slaw mixture, mixing well. Make at least 1 hour before serving.

Very different — but very good and it will last in the refrigerator for several days.

SPECIAL SPINACH SALAD

1 (10 ounce) package fresh spinach
1/2 (14 ounce) can bean sprouts
1 (8 ounce) can water chestnuts, drained and sliced
3 hard-boiled eggs, sliced
1 bunch green onions, cut up (tops too)
6 strips bacon, crisply fried and crumbled
Dressing:
1/2 cup oil
1/2 cup white vinegar
1/3 cup sugar
2 tablespoons packed brown sugar
3 tablespoons catsup
1 tablespoon Worcestershire
1/2 teaspoon salt

Wash spinach. It must be dried very well. Shake several times in dry cup towel. Remove stems from spinach and tear into small pieces. In a large bowl, combine spinach, bean sprouts, water chestnuts, eggs and onions. Toss. Add bacon just before serving. Mix dressing and pour about 1/2 of dressing over salad. That may be enough, but some may want more dressing.

CAULIFLOWER AND BROCCOLI SALAD

1 (8 ounce) carton sour cream
1 cup mayonnaise
1 package original Ranch dressing mix
1 large head cauliflower, broken into bite size pieces
1 large bunch fresh broccoli, broken into bite size pieces
1 (10 ounce) box frozen green peas, thawed, uncooked
3 stalks celery, sliced
1 bunch green onions, chopped (tops too)
1 (8 ounce) can water chestnuts, drained
1/3 cup sweet relish, drained
8 ounces mozzarella cheese, cut in chunks
2 (2.25 ounce) packages slivered almonds, toasted (page 86)

Mix together the sour cream, mayonnaise and dressing mix; set aside. MAKE SURE cauliflower and broccoli are WELL DRAINED. In a large container mix together all salad ingredients. Add dressing and toss. Refrigerate. Serves 12.

CARUSO SALAD

1/2 pound curly vegetable pasta
1 small bunch broccoli, cut into bite size pieces
2 small zucchini, sliced
1/2 red bell pepper, chopped
4 ounces pepperoni, cut into strips
8 ounces mozzarella cheese, cut in chunks
1 (6 ounce) jar artichoke hearts, cut in pieces, undrained
1 (8 ounce) jar Italian dressing

Cook pasta according to directions. Rinse in cold water. Toss together with broccoli, zucchini, bell pepper, pepperoni and cheese; mix thoroughly. Mix in the artichoke hearts, including the oil that they are in. Toss with Italian dressing. Cover and chill at least 2 hours before serving. Stir again before serving. Serves 10 to 12.

Pasta salad at its best!

VEGGIE SALAD

5 zucchini, sliced paper thin
4 yellow squash, sliced paper thin
1 head cauliflower, cut in bite size pieces
1 red bell pepper, chopped
1 bunch green onions, sliced (tops too)
2 (2 ounce) packages slivered almonds, toasted (page 86)
1/2 teaspoon salt
1/4 teaspoon black pepper
1 (8 ounce) bottle creamy Italian dressing

Mix together the zucchini, yellow squash, cauliflower, bell pepper, onions, almonds, salt and pepper. Add the dressing and toss. Refrigerate serveral hours before serving.

Crunchy and good!

ORIENTAL SALAD

1 (14 ounce) can Chinese vegetables
1 (10 ounce) package frozen Chinese pea pods,
    cooked and cut in half
1/2 red bell pepper, sliced very thin
1 bunch green onion, sliced (tops too)
1 cup chopped celery
3/4 cup slivered almonds, toasted (page 86)
1 (8 ounce) can water chestnuts
1 package Ramen noodles, broken (uncooked)
Dressing:
1/2 cup oil
3/4 cup sugar
3/4 cup white vinegar
1/2 teaspoon salt
1 1/2 teaspoon seasoned pepper
1/2 teaspoon garlic powder
Flavor packet in Ramen noodles

Combine and mix all salad ingredients in a large bowl. For the dressing, combine all ingredients and pour over salad and toss. Refrigerate several hours before serving.

BROCCOLI SALAD

1 large bunch broccoli, cut in bite size pieces
1 cup chopped celery
1 bunch green onions, sliced (tops too)
1/2 red bell pepper, chopped
1 cup seedless green grapes, sliced in half
1 cup seedless red grapes, sliced in half
1 cup slivered almonds, toasted (page 86)
1/2 pound bacon, cooked crisp, drained and crumbled
Dressing:
1 cup mayonnaise
1/4 cup sugar
2 tablespoons vinegar
1 teaspoon salt
1/2 teaspoon black pepper

Wash and drain broccoli well. It will help to drain broccoli if you will place pieces on a cup towel; pick it up and shake well. Mix all ingredients of the salad together and toss. Mix together the dressing ingredients and add to salad. Toss. Refrigerate. Serves 8 to 10.

The grapes give the recipe a special "zip".

CHERRY CRANBERRY SALAD

1 (6 ounce) package cherry gelatin
1 cup boiling water
1 can cherry pie filling
1 (16 ounce) can whole cranberry sauce

In a mixing bowl, combine cherry gelatin and boiling water; mix until gelatin is dissolved. Add pie filling and cranberry sauce. Mix well. Pour into a 7x11 inch dish and refrigerate. Serve on a lettuce leaf. Serves 6 to 8.

This is quick, easy and great!

MINCEMEAT SALAD

1 3/4 cups orange juice
1 (6 ounce) package lemon gelatin
2 cups prepared mincemeat
1 cup chopped celery
1 cup chopped pecans
1 (15 ounce) can crushed pineapple, drained
1 medium apple, diced
1 tablespoon lemon juice

Heat orange juice. Add gelatin; stir until dissolved. Stir in mincemeat, celery, pecans and pineapple. Sprinkle lemon juice over apple and toss. Add to other ingredients. Pour into a Pam sprayed 9x13 inch glass dish. Chill. Serves 12.

CREAMY FRUIT SALAD

1 can sweetened condensed milk
1/4 cup lemon juice
1 can peach pie filling*
1 (15 ounce) can pineapple chunks, drained
2 (15 ounce) cans fruit cocktail, drained
1 cup chopped pecans
1 (8 ounce) carton Cool Whip

In a large bowl, combine condensed milk and lemon juice. Stir until well mixed. Add the pie filling, pineapple chunks, fruit cocktail and pecans. Mix. Fold in Cool Whip. Serve in a pretty crystal bowl. *You can substitute any other pie filling. Serves 12 to 14.

Christmas Dinner

Turkey, Dressing and Gravy
Almond Asparagus Bake
Sweet Potato Casserole
Colorful Party Peas
Cranapple Wiggle (page 33)
Christmas Lemon Pecan Cake
(page 59)
With Whipped Cream

CHOOSING YOUR TURKEY

If you expect to serve turkey for more than one meal, allow 1 1/2 to 2 pounds per person. To serve for one meal only, allow 3/4 to 1 pound per person if the turkey weighs less than 12 pounds. Allow 1/2 to 3/4 pound per serving for turkey weighing over 12 pounds.

THAWING THE TURKEY

Place on a tray in refrigerator in original wrap. Allow 2 days for defrosting a turkey under 10 pounds. Allow 3 days for defrosting a 10 to 14 pound turkey. Allow 4 days for defrosting a 15 to 20 pound turkey. When ready to cook, remove metal clamp from legs. Run cold water into breast and neck cavities until giblets and neck can be removed. Interior should be cold to slightly icy. Refrigerate until ready to cook.

COOKING THE TURKEY

Preheat oven to 450 degrees!

Rub entire turkey with margarine and lightly salt (optional) and pepper all over. Place turkey in roaster, breast side up. Cover bottom of pan with 1/2 to 1 cup water. Place 1 or 2 stalks of celery and 1/2 peeled white onion inside the cavity. Put lid on or cover loosely with foil. Follow the cooking time chart and baste occasionally with drippings while turkey is cooking.

When ready to place turkey in the oven,
turn heat down to 325 degrees!

Weight of unstuffed turkey (pounds)	Cooking time at 325 degrees (hours)
6 to 8	3 to 3 1/2
8 to 12	3 1/2 to 4 1/2
12 to 16	4 1/2 to 5 1/2
16 to 20	5 1/2 to 6 1/2
20 to 24	6 1/2 to 7

The turkey will be done when meat thermometer in thigh registers 180 to 185 degrees or breast temperature registers 170 to 175 degrees and leg joint moves freely. About 45 minutes before turkey is scheduled to be done, remove lid and allow for final browning.

Carving the Turkey

You will need a sharp carving knife, a two tined meat fork and a serving plate for the sliced meat. Insert fork into drumstick joint, pulling the leg away from the body. Slice down until the ball and socket hip joint is exposed. To sever, make a twisting motion with the knife and continue to hold down firmly with the fork. Cut joint as shown below.

Repeat the same for cutting off the other leg. Some slices of meat may be cut for those who prefer dark meat. Proceed to remove wings in a similar manner. To slice the breast, begin at area nearest the neck and slice thinly across the grain. Slice entire length of breast. Carve only one side until more is needed.

DRESSING AND GRAVY

2 packages cornbread mix, prepared as directed
9 biscuits or 1 recipe of Bisquick biscuits, prepared as directed
1 small onion, chopped
2 celery stalks, chopped
2 eggs
Black pepper
2 teaspoons poultry seasoning
3 (14 1/2 ounce) cans chicken broth
Gravy:
2 cans chicken broth
2 heaping tablespoons cornstarch
Black pepper
2 boiled eggs, sliced (optional)

Prepare cornbread and biscuits ahead. Crumble cornbread and biscuits into a large bowl using a little more cornbread than biscuits. Add onion, celery, eggs and seasonings. Stir in 2 1/2 cans of the broth. If the mixture is not "runny", add the rest of the broth. (If it is still not runny, add a little milk.) Bake in a Pam sprayed 9x13 inch glass baking dish at 350 degrees for about 45 minutes or until golden brown. This can be frozen uncooked — just thaw before cooking.

For the gravy: In a saucepan, mix the cornstarch with a half cup of the broth — mixed with no lumps. Then add the remaining broth and heat to boiling, stirring constantly until broth thickens. Add boiled eggs.

ALMOND ASPARAGUS BAKE

5 (10 ounce) cans asparagus
1 1/2 cups cracker crumbs
4 eggs, hard-boiled and sliced
1 1/2 cups grated Cheddar cheese
1 stick margarine, melted
1/2 cup milk
2 (2.5 ounce) packages sliced almonds

Drain asparagus and arrange half the asparagus in a Pam sprayed 9x13 inch baking dish. Cover with 3/4 cup crumbs and half the sliced eggs; sprinkle with 1/2 of the cheese. Layer remaining asparagus, 3/4 cup crumbs and remaining eggs. Drizzle margarine and milk over casserole and top with almonds and the remaining cheese. Bake at 350 degrees for 30 minutes. Serves 10 to 12.

Sweet Potato Casserole

1 (29 ounce) can sweet potatoes, drained
1/3 cup evaporated milk
3/4 cup sugar
2 eggs, beaten
1/2 stick margarine, melted
1 teaspoon vanilla
Topping:
1 cup light brown sugar
1/3 cup margarine, melted
1/2 cup flour
1 cup chopped pecans

Heat oven to 350 degrees. Place sweet potatoes in a mixing bowl and mash slightly with fork. Add evaporated milk, sugar, eggs, margarine and vanilla. Mix well. Pour into a greased 7x11 inch baking dish. Mix topping ingredients together and sprinkle over top of casserole. Bake, uncovered, for 35 minutes or until crusty on top. Serves 8.

Colorful Party Peas

4 tablespoons water
1 (16 ounce) package frozen green peas
1 (6 ounce) jar sliced mushrooms
1 (4 ounce) jar chopped pimentos
1/2 stick margarine
1 can water chestnuts, drained
1 tablespoon sugar
1/2 teaspoon salt
1/4 teaspoon white pepper
3 tablespoons cornstarch
1/2 cup milk
1 jar mild Mexican Cheese Whiz

In a large saucepan, combine water, peas, mushrooms, pimentos, margarine, water chestnuts, sugar, salt and pepper. Bring to a boil and let simmer 5 to 10 minutes. In a small bowl, mix cornstarch and milk, stirring well; pour into vegetables and stir. Cook on low heat just until mixture has thickened. Leaving on low heat, add Cheese Whiz and stir just until cheese is melted. Pour into a serving bowl. Serves 8 to 10.

Delicious!

Christmas Dinner

Apricot Baked Ham
Creamy Mashed Potatoes
Cheesy Green Beans
Baked Corn
Winter Fruit Salad
Cinnamon Almond Pecan Pie (page 66)

You might choose to serve the Glazed, Spiral Sliced Ham that is so popular today. It can be served at room temperature or heated. To serve hot, preheat oven to 325 degrees and place ham on a rack, uncovered, in a shallow pan. For a whole ham cook 15 minutes per pound. For a half ham, allow about 10 minutes per pound. It would be delicious served with the Hot and Sweet Mustard sauce (page 87).

APRICOT BAKED HAM

1 (12 to 15 pound) whole ham, fully cooked,
    bone-in
Whole cloves
2 tablespoons dry mustard
1 1/4 cups apricot jam
1 1/4 cups light brown sugar

Preheat oven to 450 degrees. Trim skin and excess fat from ham. Place ham on a rack in a large roasting pan. Insert cloves in ham every inch or so. Be sure to push cloves into the ham surface as far as they will go.

Combine the dry mustard and the jam. Spread over entire surface of the ham. Pat the brown sugar over the jam mixture. Reduce heat to 325 degrees. Bake uncovered at 15 minutes per pound. The sugary crust that forms on the ham keeps the juices in. When ham is done, remove from oven and let ham set about 20 minutes before carving.

I usually buy a 10 to 12 pound "butt" end half a ham. And this crusty recipe makes it delicious!

CREAMY MASHED POTATOES

6 large potatoes
1 (8 ounce) carton sour cream
1 (8 ounce) package cream cheese, softened
1 teaspoon salt
1/2 teaspoon white pepper

This can be made the day before and reheated. Peel, cut up and boil the potatoes. Drain. Whip hot potatoes and add the sour cream, cream cheese, salt and pepper. Whip until cream cheese has melted. Pour into a greased 3 quart baking dish. Cover with foil and bake at 325 degrees for about 20 minutes. (About 10 minutes longer if you are reheating them.) Serves 8 to 10.

CHEESY GREEN BEANS

3 (16 ounce) cans green beans, drained
1 (8 ounce) can sliced water chestnuts, drained
2 (8 ounce) jars Cheese Whiz
1 cup cracker crumbs
2 cans onion rings

Place green beans in a greased 9x13 inch baking dish and cover with water chestnuts. Heat both jars of cheese in the microwave just until they can be poured. Pour Cheese Whiz over green beans and water chestnuts. Sprinkle cracker crumbs over the cheese. Arrange onion rings over the casserole and bake at 350 degrees for 30 minutes. Serves 12.

BAKED CORN

1/2 stick margarine
1 (8 ounce) package cream cheese
2 (16 ounce) packages frozen corn
1 (4 ounce) can chopped green chilies
2 stalks celery, sliced
1 bell pepper, chopped
1/2 teaspoon seasoned salt
1/2 teaspoon white pepper
1 1/2 cups crushed cracker crumbs

Melt margarine in a large saucepan and stir in cream cheese. Keep saucepan on low heat; stirring until cream cheese is melted. Add corn, green chilies, celery, bell pepper, salt and pepper. Mix and pour into a greased 9x13 inch baking dish. Sprinkle cracker crumbs over casserole. Bake at 350 degrees for 30 minutes. Serves 10.

WINTER FRUIT SALAD

2 cans mandarin oranges
2 (15 1/2 ounce) cans pineapple chunks
1 (16 ounce) carton frozen strawberries
1 can peach pie filling
1 can apricot pie filling
2 bananas, sliced

Drain oranges, pineapple and strawberries. Combine all ingredients and fold salad gently (so as not to break up any of the fruit). Chill. If you want to make a day early, mix together oranges, pineapple and pie fillings and then add the drained strawberries and bananas at the last minute. Serves 12 to 15.

Don't Throw Away the Leftovers

Jazzy Turkey and Dressing

1 (8 ounce) package stuffing
3 cups diced, cooked turkey
1 (15 ounce) can golden hominy, drained
1 (4 ounce) can chopped green chilies, drained.
1/2 cup chopped red bell pepper
2 tablespoons dried parsley flakes
1 can cream of chicken soup, undiluted
1 (8 ounce) carton sour cream
1/2 cup water
1/4 stick margarine, melted
2 teaspoons ground cumin
1/2 teaspoon salt
1 cup shredded mozzarella cheese

In a large mixing bowl, combine all ingredients except cheese. Mix well and pour into a greased 9x13 inch baking dish; cover with foil. Bake at 350 degrees for 35 minutes. Uncover; sprinkle with cheese and bake an additional 5 minutes. Serves 10 to 12.

Dorito Delight

3 1/2 cups cooked, diced turkey (or chicken)
1 (9 1/2 ounce) bag Doritos
1 onion, chopped
3 stalks celery, chopped
1 can cream of chicken soup
2 (10 ounce) cans tomatoes and green chilies
1 pound Velveeta cheese, cut in chunks

Pam spray a 9x13 inch baking dish and place 1/2 of the bag of Doritos in dish. Crush a little with the palm of your hand. In a large saucepan, combine onion, celery, chicken soup, tomatoes and green chilies and Velveeta. On medium heat, stir until cheese is melted. Add chicken pieces and pour over Doritos. Crush remaining Doritos in a baggie with a rolling pin. Sprinkle over chicken-cheese mixture. Bake at 350 degrees about 35 minutes or until bubbly around edges. Serves 8 to 10.

DIVINE TURKEY CASSEROLE

1 (16 ounce) package frozen broccoli spears
1 teaspoon seasoned salt
3 cups diced, cooked turkey (or chicken)
1 can cream of chicken soup (undiluted)
2 tablespoons milk
1/3 cup mayonnaise
2 teaspoons lemon juice
1/4 teaspoon black pepper
3 tablespoons melted margarine
1 cup bread crumbs (or cracker crumbs)
1/3 cup shredded Cheddar cheese

Cook broccoli as directed on package; drain. Place broccoli in a 8x12 inch Pam sprayed glass baking dish and sprinkle seasoned salt over the broccoli. Cover with the diced turkey. In a saucepan, combine soup, milk, mayonnaise, lemon juice and pepper. Heat just enough to dilute the soup a little; pour over the turkey. Mix melted margarine, bread crumbs and cheese and sprinkle over soup mixture. Bake uncovered in a preheated 350 degree oven for 30 minutes or until mixture is hot and bubbly. Serves 6.

CREAMY TURKEY ENCHILADAS

2 tablespoons margarine
1 onion, finely chopped
3 green onions, chopped (tops too)
1/2 teaspoon garlic powder
1/2 teaspoon seasoned salt
1 (7 ounce) can chopped green chilies
2 (8 ounce) packages of cream cheese, softened
3 cups diced turkey (or chicken)
8 (8 inch) flour tortillas
2 (8 ounce) cartons whipping cream
1 (16 ounce) package shredded Monterey Jack cheese

In a large skillet, add margarine and saute onions. Add garlic powder, seasoned salt and green chilies. Stir in cream cheese. Heat and stir until cream cheese is melted. Add diced turkey. Lay out the 8 tortillas and spoon about 3 heaping tablespoons of the turkey mixture on each tortilla. Roll up tortillas and place seam side down in a lightly greased large 9 1/2x13 1/2 inch baking dish. Pour whipping cream over enchiladas; then sprinkle the cheese over the enchiladas. Bake uncovered at 350 degrees for 35 minutes.

JALAPENO TURKEY

2 cups chopped onion
2 tablespoons margarine
1 (10 ounce) package frozen spinach, cooked and drained
6 jalapenos or 1 (7 ounce) can green chilies
1 (8 ounce) carton sour cream
2 cans cream of chicken soup
4 green onion tops, chopped
1/2 teaspoon salt
1 (12 ounce) package Doritos, slightly crushed
4 cups diced turkey (or chicken)
1 (8 ounce) package shredded Monterey Jack cheese

Saute onion in margarine. Blend in spinach, peppers, sour cream, soups, onion tops and salt. In a large 15x10 inch baking dish (or two 9x9 inch), alternate Doritos, turkey, spinach mixture and cheese. Repeat layers with the cheese on top. Bake 35 minutes at 350 degrees.

Even if you are not a spinach fan,
you will find this to your liking!

TURKEY AND HAM TETRAZZINI

1 (7 ounce) package spaghetti, cooked and drained
1/2 cup slivered almonds, toasted (page 86)
1 can cream of mushroom soup
1 can cream of chicken soup
3/4 cup milk
2 tablespoons dry white wine
2 1/2 cups diced turkey
2 cups fully cooked, diced ham
1/2 cup chopped green bell pepper
1/2 cup halved pitted ripe olives
1 (8 ounce) package shredded Cheddar cheese

Rinse cooked spaghetti with cold water to maintain firmness. Mix together almonds, soups, milk and wine in dish. Stir in spaghetti, turkey, ham, chopped pepper and pitted olives. Pour into a Pam sprayed 9x13 inch baking dish. Sprinkle top of mixture with the Cheddar cheese. Bake uncovered for 35 minutes at 350 degrees or until hot and bubbly. Serves 10.

SPICY TURKEY SOUP

3 to 4 cups chopped turkey
3 (10 ounce) cans condensed chicken broth, undiluted
2 (10 ounce) cans diced tomatoes and green chiles
1 (16 ounce) can whole corn
1 large onion, chopped
1 (10 ounce) can tomato soup
1 teaspoon garlic powder
1 teaspoon dried oregano
3 tablespoons cornstarch
3 tablespoons water

In a large roaster, combine turkey, broth, tomatoes and green chilies, corn, onion, tomato soup, garlic powder and oregano. Mix cornstarch with the water and add to soup mixture. Bring to boiling, then reduce heat and simmer, stirring occasionally about 2 hours. Yield about 2 1/2 quarts.

This is spicy — not too much — just right!

CHINESE TURKEY

3 1/2 cups cooked turkey, cut in bite size chunks
2 cans cream of chicken soup
1 (16 ounce) can Chop Suey vegetables, drained
1 (8 ounce) can sliced water chestnuts, drained
3/4 cup cashew nuts
1 cup chopped green peppers
1 bunch green onions, sliced (tops too)
1/2 cup chopped celery
1/3 teaspoon Tabasco
1/4 teaspoon curry powder
1 (5 ounce) can Chow Mein noodles

In a large bowl, combine turkey, soups, vegetables, water chestnuts, cashew nuts, green pepper, green onions, celery, Tabasco and curry powder. Stir to mix well. Spoon into a Pam sprayed 9x13 inch glass baking dish. Sprinkle Chow Mein noodles over top of casserole. Bake uncovered at 350 degrees for 30 to 35 minutes or until bubbly at edges of casserole. Let sit 5 minutes before serving. Serves 10.

MEXICAN TURKEY FIESTA

4 cups chopped turkey (or 7 chicken breast halves, cooked)
1 onion, chopped
1 (12 ounce) bag shredded Cheddar cheese
1 green bell pepper, chopped
1 teaspoon chili powder
1/2 teaspoon salt
1/2 teaspoon black pepper
1/2 teaspoon ground cumin
2 cans cream of chicken soup
1 (10 ounce) can diced green chilies and tomatoes
1 (10 ounce) bag tortilla chips

In a large pan, combine all ingredients except the tortilla chips; mixing well. Spray a 9x13 inch baking dish with Pam. Pour about two-thirds of the tortilla chips into the baking dish and crush slightly with the palm of your hand. Pour all of the turkey-cheese mixture over the crushed tortilla chips and spread out. Crush the remaining tortilla chips in a baggie and spread over casserole. Bake uncovered at 375 degrees for 40 minutes. Serves 12.

THREE CHEESE TURKEY CASSEROLE

1 (8 ounce) package egg noodles
3 quarts water
1 tablespoon salt
1 teaspoon oil
3 tablespoons margarine
3/4 cup chopped green bell pepper
1/2 cup chopped celery
1/2 cup chopped onion
1 can cream of chicken soup
1/2 cup milk
1 (6 ounce) jar whole mushrooms
1/2 teaspoon black pepper
1 (12 ounce) carton small-curd cottage cheese
4 cups diced turkey (or chicken)
1 (12 ounce) package shredded Cheddar cheese
3/4 cup freshly grated Parmesan

In a large kettle, place noodles in hot water; add salt and oil. Cook according to package instructions. Melt margarine in a skillet and saute the bell pepper, celery and onion. In a large bowl, combine noodles, sauted mixture, chicken soup, milk, mushrooms, black pepper, cottage cheese, turkey and Cheddar cheese. Pour into a Pam sprayed 9x13 inch baking dish. Top with the Parmesan cheese. Bake uncovered at 350 degrees for 40 minutes. Serves 10.

TURKEY SUPREME

1 onion, chopped
1 cup celery, sliced
3 tablespoons margarine
4 cups diced, cooked turkey
1 (6 ounce) package long grain and wild rice, cooked
   (plus seasoning packet)
1 can cream of celery soup
1 can cream of chicken soup
1 (4 ounce) jar pimentos
2 (15 ounce) cans French-style green beans, drained
1 cup slivered almonds
1 cup mayonnaise
1/2 teaspoon salt
1 teaspoon black pepper
2 1/2 cups crushed potato chips

Saute the onion and celery in the 3 tablespoons margarine. In a large saucepan, combine the onion-celery, turkey, rice, soups, pimentos, green beans, almonds, mayonnaise and seasonings. Pour into a greased 9-1/2x13-1/2 inch baking dish. (This needs a very large casserole dish). Sprinkle crushed potato chips over casserole. Bake uncovered at 350 degrees for 35 minutes or until potato chips are slightly browned.

If you want to make ahead and freeze, just wait until you are ready to cook the casserole to add the potato chips.

HAM CHOWDER

1 cup sliced celery
1/2 cup chopped onion
2 tablespoons margarine
3 cups shredded cabbage
3 1/2 cups fully cooked diced ham
2 (16 ounce) cans Mexican style stewed tomatoes, undrained
1 (15 ounce) can whole kernel corn, drained
1 (15 ounce) can whole potatoes, drained and sliced
1 can condensed chicken broth, undiluted
1 cup water
1/2 cup ketchup
1/4 cup light brown sugar
1/2 teaspoon salt
1/2 teaspoon garlic powder

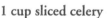

In a large roaster or soup kettle, over medium heat, saute celery and onion in the margarine. Add remaining ingredients; bring to a boil. Reduce heat; cover and simmer for 1 hour.

This is a real "tasty" way to use left-over ham — a good flavor!

PANCHO VILLA STEW

3 cups diced, cooked ham
1 pound smoked sausage (like Eckrich), cut in 1/2 inch slices
3 cans chicken broth
1 (15 ounce) can whole tomatoes, undrained
3 (4 ounce) cans chopped green chilies, undrained
1 large onion, chopped
1 teaspoon garlic powder
2 teaspoons ground cumin
2 teaspoons cocoa
1 teaspoon dried oregano
1/2 teaspoon salt
2 (15 ounce) cans pinto beans, undrained
1 (15 ounce) can hominy, undrained
1 (8 ounce) can whole kernel corn, undrained
Flour tortillas

In a roaster, combine ham, sausage, chicken broth, tomatoes, green
chilies, onion, garlic powder, cumin, cocoa, oregano and salt. Bring to a
boil, reduce heat and simmer 45 minutes. Add pinto beans, hominy
and corn, bring to a boil; reduce heat and simmer another 15 minutes.
Serve with buttered flour tortillas (or cornbread, that's good too).

CRUNCHY HAM SALAD

1 cup grated carrots
3/4 cup finely chopped celery
1/4 cup finely chopped onion
1/3 cup mayonnaise
1 teaspoon prepared mustard
1/3 cup sweet relish
1/8 teaspoon cayenne pepper (optional)
1/2 teaspoon black pepper
1 1/2 cups finely diced fully cooked ham
1 (1.5 ounce) can shoestring potato sticks

Combine the carrots, celery, onion, mayonnaise, mustard, relish,
cayenne pepper, black pepper and ham. Toss. (Add a little more
mayonnaise if salad seems too dry.) Just before serving, add the
shoestring potatoes and toss. Serves 8.

RAISIN SAUCE FOR HAM

1 1/2 cups water
1/2 teaspoon ground cloves
1 cup brown sugar
1 tablespoon corn starch
1/4 teaspoon salt
1 cup raisins
1 tablespoon margarine
1 tablespoon vinegar
1/4 teaspoon Worcestershire

In saucepan, combine water, ground cloves, brown sugar, cornstarch and salt; mixing well. Add raisins, margarine, vinegar and Worcestershire. On medium heat, bring mixture close to boiling point and quickly reduce heat and simmer for 10 to 15 minutes. Serve over ham.

CHERRY SAUCE FOR HAM

1 (16 ounce) can pitted red tart cherries, undrained
1/4 cup red wine
1/2 cup sugar
2 tablespoons corn starch
1 tablespoon lemon juice
1/4 teaspoon cinnamon

Drain the cherry juice. In a saucepan, combine cherry juice, wine, sugar, cornstarch, lemon juice and cinnamon. Cook over medium heat, stirring constantly, until mixture thickens. Add the cherries and heat. Serve over ham.

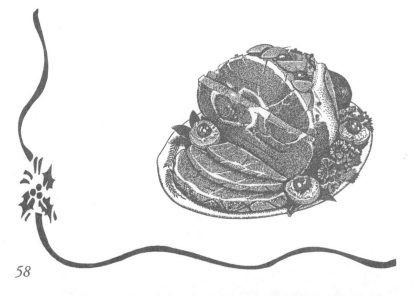

Cakes

CHRISTMAS LEMON PECAN CAKE

1 (1.5 ounce) bottle lemon
    extract
4 cups pecan halves
4 sticks butter
3 cups sugar
3 1/2 cups flour, divided
1 1/2 teaspoons baking powder

6 eggs
1/2 pound candied green
    pineapple, cut into smaller
    pieces
1/2 pound candied red
    cherries, cut in half
1/2 cup flour

Pour lemon extract over pecans in a medium bowl; toss, then set aside. Grease and flour a tube cake pan. In a large mixing bowl, cream butter and sugar until fluffy. Sift 3 cups of the flour and baking powder together in a separate bowl. Add eggs to the butter-sugar mixture, one at a time, alternately with the flour mixture. With the pineapple and cherries cut, add the 1/2 cup flour and mix so that the fruit is well covered by the flour. Fold in fruit and pecans. Pour into the tube pan and bake at 275 degrees for 2 1/2 to 2 hours and 45 minutes. Test after 2 1/2 hours for doneness. Cool and remove carefully from pan.

This cake is delicious the day you make it and still better after several days! Try it and you will want it every Christmas!

CHOCOLATE HURRICANE CAKE

1 cup chopped pecans
1 (3.5 ounce) can sweetened
    flaked coconut
1 box German chocolate cake
    mix
1 1/4 cups water
1/3 cup oil

3 eggs
1 stick margarine, melted
1 (8 ounce) package cream
    cheese, softened
1 (1 pound) box powdered
    sugar

Grease and flour a 9x13 inch baking pan. Cover the bottom of the pan with the pecans and coconut. In mixer bowl, mix together the cake mix, water, oil and eggs, beating well. Pour batter, carefully over the pecans and coconut. In mixer bowl, combine the margarine, cream cheese and powdered sugar; whip to blend. Spoon over unbaked batter. Bake at 350 degrees for 40 to 42 minutes. You cannot test for doneness with a cake tester, as the cake will appear sticky even when it is done. The icing sinks into the bottom as it bakes, forming the while ribbon inside. Makes a delicious and easy cake to make.

A light chocolate delight!

SWEET ANGEL CAKE

1 1/2 cups powdered sugar
1/2 cup milk
1 (8 ounce) package cream cheese, softened
1 (3 1/2 ounce) can coconut
1 cup chopped pecans
1 (12 ounce) carton Cool Whip
1 large angel food cake, torn into bite-size pieces
1 (16 ounce) can cherry pie filling

Add sugar and milk to the cream cheese and beat in mixer. Fold in coconut and pecans. Then stir in Cool Whip and the cake pieces. Spread in a large 9 1/2x13 1/2 inch glass dish. Chill several hours. Add pie filling by the tablespoon on top of the cake mixture. It will not cover the cake mixture, but it will just be in clumps, making a pretty red and white dessert. Refrigerate. Serves 15 to 16.

This is a super dessert you'll want — winter and summer!

APPLE DATE PECAN CAKE

2 cups sugar
1 1/2 cups oil
3 eggs
2 teaspoons vanilla
2 1/2 cups flour
1 teaspoon soda
1/2 teaspoon salt
1 1/2 teaspoons cinnamon
1/4 teaspoon ground ginger
3 cups chopped apples
1 (8 ounce) package chopped dates
1 cup chopped pecans
Glaze:
1 cup sugar
1/3 cup water
1 teaspoon almond extract

Blend together the sugar, oil, eggs and vanilla. Beat well. Add the flour, soda, salt, cinnamon and ginger; beating well. Fold in the apples, dates and pecans. Pour into a 10 inch greased and floured tube pan. Bake in a preheated oven at 325 degrees for 1 hour and 30 minutes or until cake tests done. Right before cake is done, bring sugar and water to a rolling boil. Remove from heat and add almond extract. Pour glaze over hot cake while still in pan. Let stand about 20 minutes before removing from pan.

This cake is so moist and just full of goodies!

PUMPKIN PIE POUND CAKE

1 cup Crisco
1 1/4 cups sugar
3/4 cup brown sugar
5 eggs, room temperature
1 cup canned pumpkin
2 1/2 cups flour
2 teaspoons cinnamon
1 teaspoon ground nutmeg
1/2 teaspoon mace
1/2 teaspoon salt

1 teaspoon baking soda
1/2 cup orange juice, room
    temperature
2 teaspoons vanilla
1 1/2 cups chopped pecans
Icing:
2 cups powdered sugar
3/4 stick margarine, melted
3 tablespoons orange juice
1/4 teaspoon orange extract

Cream together the shortening and sugars for about 5 minutes. Add the eggs, one at a time, mixing well after each addition. Blend in the pumpkin. In a separate bowl, mix together the flour, spices, salt and baking soda, mixing well. Gradually beat the dry ingredients into batter until well mixed. Fold in the orange juice, vanilla and chopped pecans. Pour into a greased and floured bundt pan. Bake in a preheated oven at 325 degrees for one hour and 5 to 10 minutes, or until a tester comes out clean. Allow the cake to rest in the pan for 10 to 15 minutes, then turn cake out onto a rack to cool completely before icing.

For the icing, thoroughly mix all icing ingredients together. Ice the cooled cake.

How could you miss — having pumpkin pie and pound cake all rolled up in one recipe!

FAVORITE CAKE

1 box Betty Crocker yellow cake mix
3 eggs
1 1/4 cups water
1/3 cup oil
1 box coconut pecan icing mix

In mixer bowl, combine the cake mix, eggs, water and oil. Beat well. Stir in 1 box coconut pecan icing mix; mixing well. Pour into a greased and floured bundt pan. Bake in a preheated oven at 350 degrees for 45 minutes. Test with a toothpick.

All these ingredients you can always have on hand to make hurriedly when you need to take food to friends in need! And it's good, too!

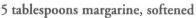

SURPRISE CAKE

5 tablespoons margarine, softened
1 package coconut pecan frosting mix
1 cup uncooked oats
1 cup sour cream
4 eggs
1 1/2 cups bananas, mashed
1 package yellow cake mix

In a saucepan, melt margarine; stir in frosting mix and rolled oats until crumbly. Set aside. In a large bowl, blend sour cream, eggs and bananas until smooth. Blend in cake mix. Beat 2 minutes and pour 2 cups of the batter into a greased and floured tube pan. Sprinkle with 1 cup of the crumb mixture. Repeat twice with batter and crumbs, ending with crumb mixture. Bake in a 350 degree preheated oven for 55 to 60 minutes. Cool in pan for 15 minutes. Remove from pan and turn cake so crumb mixture is on top.

PUMPKIN CAKE

3 eggs
2 cups sugar
1 (15 ounce) can pumpkin
1 cup oil
2 cups flour
1 teaspoon soda
2 teaspoons baking powder
2 teaspoons cinnamon
1/2 teaspoon ginger
1/2 teaspoon cloves
1/2 teaspoon nutmeg
1/2 teaspoon salt
Frosting:
1 (3 ounce) package cream cheese, softened
3/4 stick margarine, melted
3 cups powdered sugar
1 teaspoon vanilla
1 tablespoon milk

In a mixer bowl, beat together the eggs, sugar, pumpkin and oil. Add the flour, soda, baking powder, spices and salt. Mix well. Pour into a 9x13 inch greased and floured baking pan. Bake at 350 degrees for 30 to 35 minutes. Test for doneness. Mix together all frosting ingredients (add more milk if frosting is too stiff). Pour over hot cake.

CRANBERRY ALMOND CAKE

1 stick margarine, softened
1 cup sugar
2 eggs
1 teaspoon almond extract
2 cups flour
1 teaspoon baking powder
1/4 teaspoon salt
1 (8 ounce) carton sour cream

1 cup whole cranberry
  sauce
3/4 cup slivered almonds,
  chopped
Glaze:
1 1/2 cups powdered sugar
2 tablespoons milk
1/2 teaspoon almond extract

Cream margarine and sugar, beating until fluffy. Add eggs, beating after each. Add almond extract. Combine flour, baking powder and salt. Add flour mixture and sour cream, alternately to sugar mixture, beginning and ending with flour mixture. Fold in cranberry sauce and almonds. Pour batter into a greased and floured 9x13 inch baking pan. Bake in a preheated oven at 350 degrees for 30 to 35 minutes or until cake tester comes out clean. Combine glaze ingredients and drizzle over warm cake.

This is good for dessert or as a coffee cake for breakfast.

ORANGE DATE CAKE

4 cups flour
1 teaspoon soda
2 sticks margarine, softened
2 1/2 cups sugar
4 eggs
1 1/2 cups buttermilk
1 teaspoon orange extract
1 tablespoon grated orange rind
1 (11 ounce) can mandarin
  oranges

1 (8 ounce) package
  pre-chopped dates
1 cup chopped pecans
Glaze:
1/2 cup orange juice
1 1/4 cups sugar
1 teaspoon orange rind
1/2 teaspoon orange extract

Sift flour and soda together. Set aside. Cream together the margarine and sugar. Add eggs, one at a time, beating well. Add buttermilk and dry ingredients alternately, ending with dry ingredients. Add orange extract and rind; beat well. Stir in oranges, dates and pecans. Pour into a greased and floured bundt pan and bake at 350 degrees for 1 hour and 15 minutes or until cake tests done. Remove from oven and pour glaze over cake while still in pan. To make glaze, mix orange juice, sugar, orange rind and extract. Bring to boiling point; then cool.

This is so moist and good — if you don't happen to have buttermilk on hand, just put about 2 tablespoons of lemon juice in 1 1/2 cups of milk and let it set 10 or 15 minutes — presto, you'll have buttermilk.

BROWN SUGAR-RUM POUND CAKE

3 sticks butter, softened
1 (16 ounce) package brown
    sugar
1 cup sugar
5 large eggs
3/4 cup milk

1/4 cup rum
2 teaspoons vanilla
3 cups flour
2 teaspoons baking powder
1/4 teaspoon salt
1 1/2 cups chopped pecans

In the electric mixer, beat butter and sugars at medium speed about 5 minutes. Add eggs, one at a time, beating just until yellow disappears. Combine milk, rum and vanilla. Combine flour, baking powder and salt. Add half the flour mixture and mix. Add the milk mixture and mix. Add remaining flour mixture, beating at low speed. Fold in pecans. Pour into a greased and floured tube pan. Bake in a preheated 325 degree oven for 1 hour and 25 minutes. Test with a toothpick to make sure cake is done. Cool in pan for 20 minutes. Remove from pan; cool.

If you don't want to use the rum, just add another
1/4 cup of milk and 2 teaspoons of rum flavoring.

RED VELVET POUND CAKE

3 cups sugar
3/4 cup shortening
6 eggs
1 teaspoon vanilla
1/4 teaspoon salt
3 cups flour
1 cup milk
2 (1 ounce) bottles red food
    coloring

Icing:
1 (1 pound) box powdered
    sugar
1 (3 ounce) package cream
    cheese, softened
1/2 stick margarine, softened
3 tablespoons milk
Red sprinkles

Cream sugar and shortening together. Add eggs one at a time, beating after each addition. Add vanilla, mix. Add salt, flour and milk alternately beginning and ending with flour. Add food coloring; beat until smooth. Bake in a greased and floured tube pan at 325 degrees for 1 hour and 30 minutes or until cake tests done. Let cake rest in the pan for 10 minutes. Take cake out of pan and let cool completely.

Frost. To make icing, cream together the powdered sugar, cream cheese, margarine and milk; mix well. Ice cake and top with a few red sprinkles over the white icing.

So pretty and kids love it! The icing and color make this an
extra special pound cake.

Pies

ANGEL DUST PIE

3 egg whites
1 cup Ritz cracker crumbs
Pinch of salt
1 1/4 cups sugar
2 teaspoons vanilla (divided)
3/4 cup chopped pecans
1 cup whipping cream
1/4 cup powdered sugar
1 cube white chocolate, grated (white almond bark)

Beat egg whites to **very stiff** peaks. Combine cracker crumbs, salt, sugar, 1 teaspoon vanilla and pecans. Fold into beaten egg whites. spread in a buttered and floured 9 inch pie plate. Bake at 325 degrees for 45 minutes. Cool completely. Whip cream with powdered sugar and 1 teaspoon vanilla. Spread over crust. Sprinkle grated white chocolate over whipped cream. Refrigerate.

A favorite at our "testing" party!

CHRISTMAS FRUIT PIE

1 (16 ounce) can tart red cherries, drained (save juice)
1 (15 ounce) can crushed pineapple, drained (save juice)
Water
8 tablespoons cornstarch
2 1/2 cups sugar
1/2 teaspoon salt
3 teaspoons red food coloring
1 cup chopped pecans
2 bananas, mashed
2 (9 inch) graham cracker pie crusts
1 (8 ounce) carton Cool Whip

Add enough water to fruit juice to make 2 cups. Add fruit to juice. Mix cornstarch and sugar. Add to fruit along with salt and food coloring (add more red coloring if the fruit isn't very red). Cook until thick, stirring constantly. Cool. Add pecans and bananas. Pour into the 2 pie crusts. Divide the Cool Whip and spread on both pies.

This pie is better eaten the day or day after it is made; so if you don't need both pies, freeze one.

CINNAMON ALMOND PECAN PIE

1 (9 inch) unbaked pie shell
2/3 cup sugar
1 tablespoon flour
2 1/2 teaspoons cinnamon
4 eggs, lightly beaten
1 cup light corn syrup
2 tablespoons margarine, melted
1 tablespoon vanilla
1 1/2 teaspoons almond extract
1 cup coarsely chopped pecans
1/2 cup slivered almonds

Stir together the sugar and flour. Add the cinnamon, eggs, corn syrup, margarine, vanilla and almond extract; mixing well. Stir in chopped pecans and slivered almonds. Pour filling into the pie shell. Tear off three 1 1/2 inch strips of foil. Cover the crust with these strips (crimp a little where foil pieces come together); it will keep the crust from getting too brown. Bake 10 minutes at 400 degrees, then reduce heat to 325 degrees and bake 40 to 45 minutes more or until pie will just barely shake in center. Cool completely before serving.

A little change from the traditional pecan pie, but a good one!

ALMOND MOCHA PIE

3 (1.65 ounce) chocolate bars
3 teaspoons instant coffee
1 1/2 cups miniature marshmallows
1/2 cup milk
1/4 cup almond liqueur (Amaretto)
1 cup whipping cream, whipped
1/4 cup powdered sugar
1 graham cracker pie crust
1/3 cup finely chopped almonds, toasted (page 86)

Break candy bars in pieces. Combine chocolate, instant coffee, marshmallows and milk in a 1 quart glass bowl. Microwave on 70 percent power 3 to 4 minutes, stirring after 2 minutes; then check to see if it needs 1 or 2 more minutes. Mix until smooth. Cool completely and stir in liqueur. Chill in refrigerator until it begins to thicken. Add powdered sugar to whipped cream and fold into marshmallow mixture. Pour into pie shell. Garnish with toasted almonds. Freeze. This pie can be cut easily right out of freezer.

Lemon Pecan Chess Pie

2 1/4 cups sugar
2 tablespoons flour
1 tablespoon cornmeal
4 eggs, lightly beaten
2 tablespoons grated lemon rind
1/4 cup lemon juice
3/4 cup chopped pecans
1 unbaked pie crust

Combine sugar, flour and cornmeal in a large bowl. Toss lightly. Add eggs, lemon rind and the lemon juice. Mix until smooth and thoroughly blended. Add pecans to mixture and pour into the pie crust. Tear off three 1 1/2 inch strips of foil. Cover the crust with these strips (crimp a little where foil pieces come together); it will keep the crust from getting too brown. Bake at 400 degrees for 10 minutes. Turn oven temperature down to 325 degrees and bake 40 to 45 minutes or until center is not shaky.

Kahlua Pecan Pie

2 tablespoons margarine, melted
1 cup sugar
1 teaspoon vanilla
3 tablespoons flour
3 eggs
1/3 cup Kahlua
1/2 cup white corn syrup
1 cup chopped pecans
1 (9 inch) unbaked pie shell

Melt margarine in a large bowl. Add sugar, vanilla and flour. Mix well; add eggs and beat a few minutes by hand. Pour in Kahlua and corn syrup; mix. Place pecans in pie shell and pour sugar-egg mixture over pecans. Tear off three 1 1/2 inch strips of foil. Cover the crust with these strips (crimp a little where two pieces of foil come together); it will keep the crust from getting too brown. Bake 10 minutes at 400 degrees, then reduce heat to 325 degrees and bake 40 to 45 minutes more or until pie will just barely shake in center. Cool completely before serving.

PUMPKIN CHIFFON PIE

1 envelope Knox gelatin
1/4 cup cold water
3 eggs
1 cup sugar (divided)
1 1/4 cups pumpkin
2/3 cup milk
1/2 teaspoon ginger
1/2 teaspoon nutmeg
1/2 teaspoon cinnamon
1/2 teaspoon salt
1 baked pie crust

Soften gelatin in cold water. Set aside. Separate eggs and set whites aside. Beat yolks slightly; add 1/2 cup sugar, pumpkin, milk, spices and salt. Cook in double boiler until custard consistency, stirring constantly. Mix in softened gelatin and dissolve in hot custard. Cool. Beat egg whites, gradually adding the other 1/2 cup sugar. Fold in stiffly beaten egg whites into cooled pumpkin mixture. Turn into cooked pie crust. Refrigerate several hours before slicing.

PISTACHIO LIME PIE

2 cups vanilla wafer crumbs
1/4 cup chopped pistachio nuts (or pecans)
1/4 cup margarine, melted
1 (8 ounce) package cream cheese, softened
1 can Eagle Brand sweetened condensed milk
1/4 cup lime juice from concentrate
1 (3 ounce) package instant pistachio pudding mix
1/2 cup chopped pistachio nuts (or pecans)
1 (8 ounce) can crushed pineapple, undrained
1 (8 ounce) carton Cool Whip

Combine crumbs, 1/4 cup nuts and margarine and press firmly on bottom of a 9 inch springform pan. Bake 8 to 10 minutes and cool. In a large mixing bowl, beat cheese until fluffy and gradually beat in sweetened condensed milk and then the lime juice and pudding mix and beat until smooth. Stir in 1/2 cup nuts and pineapple and fold in Cool Whip. Pour into the springform pan and chill overnight. Keep refrigerated.

A bridge club favorite!

APRICOT COBBLER

1 can apricot pie filling
1 (20 ounce) can crushed pineapple, undrained
1 cup chopped pecans
1 yellow cake mix
2 sticks margarine, melted
Cool Whip

Spray a 9x13 inch baking dish with Pam. Pour the apricot pie filling in the pan and spread out. Then spoon the crushed pineapple and juice over the pie filling. Sprinkle the pecans over the pineapple; then sprinkle the cake mix over the pecans. Pour the melted margarine over the cake mix and bake at 375 degrees for 40 minutes or until lightly brown and crunchy. To serve, top with Cool Whip. Serves 10.

A bridge partner had this recently and everybody gave this a "blue ribbon".

WHITE CHOCOLATE PIE

9 inch pie shell, baked
4 ounces white chocolate (white almond bark)
28 large marshmallows
1/2 cup milk
1 (8 ounce) carton Cool Whip
1/2 cup chopped pecans
1 cup maraschino cherries, chopped and well drained

Melt together in a double boiler the white chocolate, marshmallows and milk. Cool. To the cooled white chocolate mixture, add the Cool Whip, pecans and cherries. Pour into pie shell and freeze. Take out of freezer 5 to 10 minutes before serving.

CREAMY LEMON PIE

1 (8 ounce) package cream cheese, softened
1 can sweetened condensed milk
1/4 cup lemon juice
1 can lemon pie filling
1 (9 inch) graham cracker pie crust

In mixing bowl, cream cheese until creamy. Add sweetened condensed milk and lemon juice. Beat until mixture is very creamy. Fold in lemon pie filling; stirring well. Pour into pie crust. Refrigerate several hours before slicing and serving.

Lemony and creamy — a good combination!

DATE PECAN TARTS

1 (8 ounce) package chopped dates
2 1/2 cups milk
1/2 cup flour
1 1/2 cups sugar
3 eggs
1/2 teaspoon salt
1 teaspoon vanilla
1 cup chopped pecans
8 tart shells, baked and cooled
1 (8 ounce) carton whipping cream
3 tablespoons powdered sugar

In a saucepan, cook dates, milk, flour and sugar until thick, stirring constantly. Add beaten eggs and salt. Cook this mixture about 5 minutes on medium heat; stirring constantly. Stir in vanilla and pecans. Pour into the tart shells. Cool. Whip cream and add powdered sugar.

This is an old-time favorite!

STRAWBERRY FLUFF

2 sticks margarine, softened
1/2 cup brown sugar
2 cups flour
1 1/2 cups chopped pecans
2 egg whites
1 tablespoon lemon juice
1 cup sugar
2 (10 ounce) packages sweetened strawberries, thawed
1 tablespoon vanilla
1 (12 ounce) carton Cool Whip

Combine and mix together the margarine, brown sugar and flour until crumbly. Add pecans and spread on a cookie sheet. Bake at 350 degrees about 15 minutes. Spread this crumbly mixture in a **large** 9 1/2x13 1/2 inch glass casserole dish. Cool. In mixer bowl, beat the egg whites for 5 minutes, then add the lemon juice, 1 cup sugar and both packages of strawberries and beat another **15 minutes**. This mixture will grow and grow and grow! Fold in the Cool Whip and pour over the crumbly crust mixture. Freeze.

This is one of the lightest, fluffiest, most delicious desserts you will ever eat! I talked a good friend out of this recipe.

Cookies

Reindeer's Rapture

3/4 cup brown sugar
3/4 cup white sugar
1 1/2 cups shortening
2 large eggs
1 1/2 cups flour
1/2 teaspoon baking soda
1/2 teaspoon salt
2 3/4 cups oats
1/2 cup chopped pecans
1/2 cup peanut butter
1 1/2 teaspoons vanilla
1 (6 ounce) package chocolate chips

Cream together sugars and shortening. Add eggs and beat. Sift together flour, soda and salt. Add to creamed mixture. Stir in oats, pecans, peanut butter, vanilla and chocolate chips. Drop by teaspoon on a cookie sheet. Bake at 350 degrees for 12 to 14 minutes or until cookies begin to brown on the edge.

Snappy Oats

3 cups quick rolled oats
1 cup chocolate chips
1/2 cup coconut
1/2 cup chopped pecans
2 cups sugar
1 1/2 sticks margarine
1/2 cup evaporated milk

Mix oats, chocolate chips, coconut and pecans in a large bowl. Bring sugar, margarine and milk to a rapid boil and boil 1 1/2 minutes, stirring constantly. Pour hot mixture over mixture in bowl and stir until chocolate chips melt. Drop by teaspoon on waxed paper. Cool at room temperature. Store in covered container.

"Snappy" because you can make these and
not even heat up the oven!

MINCEMEAT COOKIES

2 sticks margarine, softened
1 2/3 cups sugar
3 eggs, beaten
1 teaspoon soda
2 teaspoons hot water
1/2 teaspoon salt
3 1/4 cups flour
1 1/4 cups chopped pecans
1 cup prepared mincemeat

Grease cookie sheets. Cream margarine and add sugar gradually. Add eggs and then soda dissolved in water. Mix, add salt and the flour to creamed mixture. Mix well. Add pecans and mincemeat. Drop by teaspoon on cookie sheets. Bake at 350 degrees for 14 to 15 minutes or until cookies begin to brown.

For you "baby boomers" who don't know how good mincemeat is, don't overlook this recipe — it's great!

CHERRY PECAN SLICES

2 cups powdered sugar
2 sticks margarine, softened
1 egg
2 tablespoons milk
1 teaspoon vanilla
2 1/4 cups flour
2 cups whole candied red cherries
1 cup chopped pecans

In mixer bowl, cream together the sugar and margarine until slightly fluffy. Add the egg, milk and vanilla; mix. Beat in the flour. Batter will be stiff. Stir in cherries and pecans; mix well. Chill dough 1 hour. Sprinkle a tiny bit of flour on a sheet of waxed paper. Shape dough into two 10 inch rolls and wrap in waxed paper. Chill at least 3 hours or overnight. Cut rolls into 1/4 inch slices. Place on ungreased cookie sheets. Bake at 375 degrees for 10 to 12 minutes. Check cookies in 10 minutes; edges should be slightly brown. Cool on wire racks and store in a covered container.

A cherry lover's delight!

Macadamia Nut Cookies

1/2 cup shortening
1 stick margarine, softened
2 1/2 cups flour
1 cup packed brown sugar
1/2 cup granulated sugar
2 eggs
1 teaspoon vanilla
1/2 teaspoon butter flavoring
1/2 teaspoon baking soda
2 cups white chocolate chips
1 (3 1/2 ounce) jar Macadamia nuts, chopped

In mixing bowl, beat shortening and margarine. Add half of flour and mix well. Add brown sugar, granulated sugar, eggs, vanilla, butter flavoring and baking soda. Beat until mixture is well combined. Add remaining flour. Mix well and stir in chocolate pieces and nuts. Drop dough by teaspoon onto ungreased cookie sheet. Bake at 350 degrees for about 8 minutes.

Just like those good cookies you buy at the mall.

Dreamy Date Balls

1 stick margarine
1 cup sugar
1 (8 ounce) box chopped dates
1 cup Rice Crispies
1 cup chopped pecans
1 teaspoon vanilla
Powdered sugar

In a large saucepan, combine margarine, sugar and chopped dates. Cook on medium heat, stirring, until all ingredients are melted and well blended. Remove from heat; add Rice Crispies, chopped pecans and vanilla. Stir to mix well. Roll into balls about 3/4 inch in diameter. Drop balls, a few at a time, into a small grocery sack or plastic bag with enough powdered sugar to cover. Shake lightly until date balls are coated with sugar. Store in an airtight container. These can also be frozen for later use.

HOLLY ALMOND COOKIES

2 sticks margarine, softened
1 (3 ounce) package cream cheese, softened
1 1/2 cups powdered sugar
2 cups flour
1 cup almonds, very finely chopped
2 teaspoons almond flavoring
1 teaspoon vanilla
1/2 pound whole candied cherries

Cream margarine, cream cheese and sugar together. Add flour and mix well. Stir in almonds, almond flavoring and vanilla. Mix well. Take a spoon of dough and form a ball with your hands. Punch a candied cherry down in the center of each ball (not to cover the cherry, just to flatten the cookie slightly). Bake at 325 degrees for 20 to 25 minutes; the edges should be just barely browned.

FRUIT BALLS

1 1/2 pounds candied cherries
1/2 pound candied pineapple
1 (8 ounce) box pitted dates
1 (4 ounce) can angel flake coconut
4 cups chopped pecans
1 can Eagle Brand condensed milk

Chop cherries, pineapple and dates. Mix well by hand. Add coconut and pecans; then pour Eagle Brand condensed milk over mixture. Mix well. Put 1 teaspoon of mixture in miniature paper cups and place on a cookie sheet. Bake in a preheated oven at 300 degrees for 20 to 25 minutes. Store in a covered container. Makes 150 to 200 fruit balls.

These will keep in refrigerator for months if you can keep the family from eating them! My friend says it's not Christmas unless she makes these!

Jingle Bell Cookies

1 cup sugar
1 stick margarine
1/2 cup evaporated milk
1 1/2 cups small marshmallows
1 1/2 cups graham cracker crumbs (or vanilla wafers)
1 cup chopped pecans

Combine sugar, margarine and evaporated milk in saucepan. Boil for 6 minutes, stirring constantly. Remove from heat and add marshmallows, stirring until marshmallows have melted. Stir in graham cracker crumbs and pecans. Hand beat until slightly cool and mixture becomes fairly stiff. Then quickly drop by tablespoon onto buttered waxed paper to cool. Store in a covered container.

Almost like candy!

Gum Drop Chews

1 cup flour
1/2 teaspoon baking powder
1/2 teaspoon soda
1/8 teaspoon salt
1 egg
1/2 cup brown sugar
1/2 cup granulated sugar
1 stick margarine, softened
1 teaspoon vanilla
2 cups gum drops, cut up
1 cup oats
1 cup chopped pecans

In mixer, combine flour, baking powder, soda and salt. Add egg, sugars, margarine and vanilla; mixing well with dry ingredients. Add gum drops, oats and pecans; mix. Drop by teaspoon on cookie sheet. Bake for 12 to 15 minutes at 350 degrees. For a variation, use orange slices in place of gum drop.

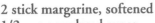

ALMOND FUDGE SHORTBREAD

2 stick margarine, softened
1/2 cup powdered sugar
1/4 teaspoon salt
1 1/4 cups flour
1 (12 ounce) package chocolate chips
1 (14 ounce) can sweetened condensed milk
1/2 teaspoon almond extract
1 (2 1/2 ounce) package almonds, toasted (page 86)

Preheat oven to 350 degrees. Grease a 9x13 inch baking pan. In mixer bowl, beat together the margarine, sugar and salt. Stir in flour. Pat into the prepared pan and bake for 15 minutes. In a medium saucepan, over low heat, melt chocolate chips with the sweetened condensed milk, stirring constantly until chips are melted. Stir in almond extract. Spread evenly over shortbread and sprinkle with almonds. Refrigerate several hours or until firm. Cut into bars. They may be stored at room temperature.

CHRISTMAS COOKIES

2 sticks margarine, softened
3/4 cup sugar
1 cup packed brown sugar
1 teaspoon vanilla
2 eggs
2 1/2 cups flour
1 teaspoon baking soda
1/2 teaspoon salt
1 (12 ounce) package white chocolate chips
1 cup chopped pecans
1 (3 1/2 ounce) can coconut
20 red candied cherries, chopped
20 green candied cherries, chopped

In a mixing bowl, cream together the margarine, sugars, vanilla and eggs. Beat well. Add flour, baking soda and salt. Mix well. Stir in chocolate chips, pecans, coconut and cherries. Drop dough by teaspoon onto an ungreased cookie sheet. Bake in a preheated 350 degree oven for 8 to 10 minutes. Cool before storing.

Holiday Spritz Cookies

1 1/4 sticks margarine, softened
1 1/4 cups sugar
1 egg, well beaten
1 teaspoon almond flavoring
Food coloring (optional)
3 cups flour
1 teaspoon baking powder

Cream margarine and sugar with mixer, then add beaten egg and almond flavoring. Beat well. If adding food coloring, add at this point. Stir flour and baking powder into creamed mixture. Place dough in a cookie press and press out desired shapes onto ungreased baking sheets. Bake at 350 degrees for about 8 minutes or until lightly browned. Use some of the decorative icings or sprinkles found in the grocery store to decorate your cookies.

Choc-O Cherry Cookies

1 stick margarine, softened
1 cup sugar
1 egg
1/2 teaspoon vanilla
1 1/2 cups flour
1/2 cup cocoa
1/4 teaspoon salt
1/4 teaspoon baking powder
1/4 teaspoon baking soda
1 (10 ounce) jar maraschino cherries, well drained
1 (6 ounce) package chocolate chips

Cream margarine, sugar, egg and vanilla until light and fluffy. Add dry ingredients and mix. Cut cherries in fourths and add cherries and chocolate chips; mix. Drop by teaspoon on a cookie sheet and bake at 350 degrees for 15 minutes.

A chocolate lover's delight!

CHRISTMAS CUT OUTS

6 tablespoons margarine, softened
1 cup sugar
2 eggs
1 teaspoon vanilla
2 1/2 cups flour
1 teaspoon baking powder
1 teaspoon salt
Powdered sugar for rolling dough

In a large mixing bowl, combine margarine, sugar, eggs and vanilla. Beat until well blended and light and fluffy. Add flour, baking powder and salt. Beat until all ingredients are well mixed. Cover and chill dough in refrigerator one hour. Sprinkle powdered sugar on counter (cookies will not toughen as they are likely to do when rolled in flour). Roll dough 1/8 inch thick and cut into desired shapes. Bake at 375 degrees for 6 to 8 minutes. Remove immediately from cookie sheet and let cool before decorating.

There is a wide variety of decorative icings already available on the grocery shelves. Many are in the tube so that even the smallest of children can quickly become an artist. Use your imagination!

ORANGE FINGERS

3 1/4 cups vanilla wafer crumbs
1 (16 ounce) box powdered sugar
2 cups chopped pecans
1 (6 ounce) can frozen orange juice concentrate, thawed and
    undiluted
1 stick margarine, melted
1 cup flaked coconut

Mix vanilla wafer crumbs, powdered sugar and pecans together. Stir in orange juice and margarine. Shape into 2 inch fingers and roll in coconut. Refrigerate. Lovely for a fancy party!

ALMOND SQUARES SPECTACULAR

2 cups graham cracker crumbs
3 tablespoons brown sugar
1 stick margarine, melted
1 (14 ounce) can sweetened condensed milk
1 (7 ounce) package coconut
1 teaspoon vanilla
Topping:
1 (6 ounce) package chocolate chips
1 (6 ounce) package butterscotch chips
4 tablespoons margarine
6 tablespoons chunky peanut butter
1/2 cup slivered almonds

Mix graham cracker crumbs, brown sugar and margarine. Pat into a greased 9x13 inch baking pan. Bake in a preheated 325 degree oven for 10 minutes. Cool. Combine sweetened condensed milk, coconut and vanilla. Pour over baked crust and bake another 25 minutes. Cool. For the topping, melt topping ingredients in top of double boiler. Spread over baked ingredients. Cool and cut into squares. Makes 3 dozen.

You'll think you're eating candy!

CANDIED GINGERBREAD

1 1/2 cups flour
1 teaspoon baking soda
1 teaspoon ground ginger
1 teaspoon cinnamon
1 stick margarine, softened
3/4 cup firmly packed brown sugar
2 eggs
1/4 cup dark molasses
2/3 cup buttermilk
1/4 cup chopped crystallized ginger

Grease and flour an 8 inch cake pan (or 9 inch square pan). Sift together flour, baking soda and spices. Set aside. Beat margarine until light and fluffy, then add sugar and beat again. Add eggs, beating well, followed by the molasses. Stir half of dry ingredients into mixture and beat; then the buttermilk; beat. Add remaining dry ingredients. Fold in crystallized ginger. Pour batter into prepared pan and bake about 45 minutes or until a tester inserted comes out clean. Cut in squares. Serve warm with butter.

The crystallized ginger is a fabulous addition
to an old-time favorite!

COCONUT CHERRY SQUARES

Pastry:
1 1/3 cups flour
1 1/4 sticks margarine, softened
1 1/2 cups powdered sugar
Filling:
3 eggs, beaten
1 1/2 cups sugar
3/4 cup flour
1/2 teaspoon salt
3/4 teaspoon baking powder
1 teaspoon vanilla
3/4 cup chopped pecans
3/4 cup coconut
3/4 cup maraschino cherries, drained and chopped

In mixer bowl, combine pastry ingredients and press into bottom of a 9x13 inch baking pan. Bake at 350 degrees for 20 minutes or just until golden. Set aside. Using the same mixer bowl, combine filling ingredients; mixing well. Spread over crust. Bake 25 minutes or until golden brown. Cool and cut into squares. You could give this an even more holiday look by using half green and half red maraschino cherries.

This is not only pretty — it's good, good, good!

PUMPKIN CRUNCH

1 (16 ounce) can pumpkin
1 cup sugar
1 tablespoon pumpkin pie spice
3 eggs
1/2 teaspoon salt
1 (12 ounce) can evaporated milk
1 yellow cake mix
1 stick margarine, melted
1 cup chopped pecans

In mixer bowl, combine pumpkin, sugar, pie spice, eggs, salt and evaporated milk. Beat well. Pour into a well greased and floured 9x13 inch baking dish. Mix together the cake mix, melted margarine and pecans; this will be a crumbly mixture. Spoon cake mixture over the pumpkin mixture. Bake in a preheated 350 degree oven for 35 to 40 minutes. This is good served warm or cold.

I talked a bridge "buddy" out of this good recipe.

APRICOT ALMOND BARS

1 package yellow cake mix
1 stick margarine, melted
3/4 cup finely chopped almonds
1 (12 ounce) jar apricot preserves (divided)
1 8 ounce) package cream cheese, softened
1/4 cup sugar
2 tablespoons flour
1/8 teaspoon salt
1 egg
1 teaspoon vanilla
2/3 cup flaked coconut

In a large bowl, combine cake mix and margarine; mix by hand just until crumbly. Stir in almonds and reserve 1 cup crumb mixture. Lightly press remaining crumb mixture into a greased 9x13 inch baking pan. Carefully spread 1 cup of the preserves over crumb mixture, leaving a 1/4 inch border. Beat cream cheese in mixer until smooth; add remaining preserves, sugar, flour, salt, egg, and vanilla; beating well. Carefully spread cream cheese mixture over top of preserves. Combine the 1 cup reserved crumb mixture and the coconut; mixing well. Sprinkle over cream cheese mixture. Bake at 350 degrees for 35 minutes or until center is set. Cool. Store in refrigerator.

ICED PINEAPPLE SQUARES

1 1/2 cups sugar
2 cups flour
1 1/2 teaspoons soda
1/2 teaspoon salt
1 (20 ounce) can crushed pineapple, undrained
2 eggs
Icing:
1 1/2 cups sugar
1 stick margarine
1 small can evaporated milk
1 cup chopped pecans
1 can coconut
1 teaspoon vanilla

Mix first 6 ingredients and pour in a 9x13 inch greased and floured pan. Bake at 350 degrees for about 35 minutes. Start cooking icing as the squares are baking. Mix sugar, margarine and evaporated milk together in a saucepan and boil 4 minutes, stirring constantly. Remove from heat and add the pecans, coconut and vanilla. Spread over hot squares. Serves 12.

GLAZED BUTTERSCOTCH BROWNIES

3 cups brown sugar
2 sticks margarine, softened
3 eggs
3 cups flour
2 tablespoons baking powder
1/2 teaspoon salt
1 1/2 cups chopped pecans
1 cup coconut
Glaze:
1/2 cup brown sugar, packed
1/3 cup evaporated milk
1 stick margarine
1/8 teaspoon salt
1 cup powdered sugar
1/2 teaspoon vanilla

Combine and beat sugar and margarine until fluffy; add eggs and blend. Sift flour, baking powder and salt together and add to the other mixture 1 cup at a time. Add pecans and coconut. Spread batter into a large 11x17 inch well greased pan and bake at 350 degrees for 20 to 25 minutes. (Batter will be hard to spread.) For glaze: In a saucepan, combine the brown sugar, milk, margarine and salt and bring to a boil. Cool slightly and add powdered sugar and vanilla and beat until smooth. Spread over cooled brownies.

BUTTER PECAN TURTLE BARS

2 cups flour
3/4 cup packed light brown sugar
1 stick margarine, softened
1 1/2 cups slightly chopped pecans
1 cup packed light brown sugar
1 1/3 sticks margarine
5 squares semi-sweet chocolate
1/2 stick margarine

In a large mixing bowl, combine flour, 3/4 cup brown sugar and margarine; blend until crumbly. Pat firmly into a greased 9x13 inch baking pan. Sprinkle pecans over unbaked crust. Set aside. In a small saucepan, combine the 1 cup brown sugar and 1 1/3 sticks margarine. Cook over medium heat, stirring constantly. When mixture comes to a boil, boil for 1 minute, stirring constantly. Drizzle this caramel sauce over pecans and crust. Bake at 350 degrees for 18 minutes or until caramel layer is bubbly. Remove from oven and cool. In a saucepan, melt chocolate squares and margarine and stir until smooth. Pour over bars and spread around. Cool and cut into bars. Refrigerate.

Candies & Specialties

SANTA'S FAVORITE FUDGE

4 1/2 cups sugar
1 (12 ounce) can evaporated milk
2 sticks margarine
3 (6 ounce) packages chocolate chips
1 tablespoon vanilla
1 1/2 cups chopped pecans

Bring sugar and milk to a rolling boil that cannot be stirred down. Boil for exactly 6 minutes, stirring constantly. Remove from heat, add margarine and chocolate chips; stir until margarine and chips have melted. Add the vanilla and pecans; stir well. Pour into a buttered 9x13 inch dish; let stand at least 6 hours or overnight before cutting. Store in a tight container.

DIVINITY

2 1/2 cups sugar
1/2 cup light corn syrup
1/2 cup water
1/4 teaspoon salt
2 egg whites
1 teaspoon vanilla
1 cup chopped pecans

Mix sugar, corn syrup, water and salt in a 2 quart saucepan. Cook over medium heat, stirring constantly, until mixture comes to boil. Reduce heat, cook, without stirring, until temperature reaches 265 degrees or until small amount of syrup forms a ball in cold water that holds its shape, yet pliable. Just before temperature reaches 265 degrees, beat egg whites in a large bowl until stiff peaks form when beater is raised. Beating constantly on high speed of electric mixer, very slowly pour hot syrup over egg whites. Continue beating until small amount holds soft peak when dropped from a spoon. Mix in vanilla and pecans. Work hurriedly and drop by teaspoon onto waxed paper. It's better to wait for a sunny day to make divinity.

DATE NUT LOAF CANDY

6 cups sugar
1 (12 ounce) can evaporated milk
1/2 cup white corn syrup
2 sticks margarine
2 (8 ounce) boxes chopped dates
3 cups chopped pecans (or English walnuts)
1 tablespoon vanilla

In a large saucepan, cook the sugar, milk, corn syrup and margarine until it boils about 5 minutes, stirring constantly with a wooden spoon or plastic spoon so the mixture will not scorch. Add dates and cook until it forms a soft ball in a cup of cold water. Take candy off the heat and beat until it begins to get thick. Add the pecans and vanilla and stir until real thick. Then spoon it out on a wet cup towel to make a roll. This will make 2 rolls of candy. Let it stay wrapped until it is firm enough to slice.

Absolutely delicious! My good friend has made this for so many years, she just "dumped" the ingredients in — without measuring! So she made up a special "batch" and actually measured everything — just for this book!

PATIENCE

1 cup milk
2 cups sugar
1 cup sugar
2 tablespoons margarine
1 teaspoon vanilla
1 cup chopped pecans

Heat milk and 2 cups sugar together in a saucepan. Caramelize the other cup of sugar in a skillet. Combine caramelized sugar with other mixture and cook until a soft ball forms in cold water. Add margarine and vanilla. Let set in pan until slightly cool. Beat until the candy is dull. Add pecans. Pour into a buttered pan or drop by teaspoon. Do not try to make on a damp day.

Our Mom make this — so it's a special recipe!

MACADAMIA CANDY

2 (3 ounce) jars Macadamia nuts
1 (20 ounce) package of white almond bark
3/4 cup coconut

Heat a dry skillet over medium heat. Toast nuts until slightly golden. Set aside. In a double boiler, melt the 9 squares of white almond bark. (If you don't have a double boiler, just use a skillet to put the water in and place the white almond bark in a saucepan.) As soon as the almond bark is melted, pour in the Macadamia nuts and coconut. Stir well. Place a piece of waxed paper on a cookie sheet and pour the candy on the waxed paper; spread out. Refrigerate 30 minutes to set. Break into pieces to serve.

This is good, good, good!

CREAMY PRALINES

2 1/4 cups sugar
1 (3 ounce) can evaporated milk
1/2 cup white corn syrup
1/4 teaspoon baking soda
1/2 stick margarine
1 teaspoon vanilla
2 cups pecans

In a double boiler, combine sugar, evaporated milk, corn syrup and baking soda. Cook, stirring constantly until balls are formed when dropped into a cup of cold water, or until it reaches the soft ball stage on a candy thermometer. This will take about 15 minutes. Remove from heat; add margarine, vanilla and pecans and beat until it is cool and stiff enough to keep its shape when dropped on wax paper.

TOASTED ALMONDS

Place almonds in a baking pan. Preheat oven to 275 degrees. Bake almonds for 15 minutes.

This can be done in advance and frozen. Nice to have on hand.

CHOCOLATE DIPPED STRAWBERRIES

1 (6 ounce) package milk chocolate chips
1 tablespoon shortening
1 pint large strawberries with stems

Wash, dry and chill the strawberries. Melt chocolate chips and shortening in top of double boiler over hot water. Stir until smooth. Hold each strawberry by the stem and dip 3/4 of the way into the chocolate. Place dipped strawberries on wax paper lined baking sheet. Refrigerate. These may be kept in refrigerator up to 4 hours before serving.

POPCORN BALLS

3 quarts popcorn (popped)
1 cup sugar
1/2 cup water
1/3 cup light corn syrup
1/2 teaspoon salt
1 teaspoon vinegar
1/2 teaspoon vanilla
Green or red food coloring (optional)

Boil sugar, water, corn syrup, salt and vinegar until the hard ball stage. Add desired food coloring and vanilla. Stir well. Pour over popcorn. Butter hands lightly and shape into balls. Wrap each in plastic wrap.

Oat Munchies

1 (16 ounce) package Quaker Oat Squares
2 cups whole pecans
1/2 cup corn syrup
1/2 cup brown sugar
1/2 stick margarine
1 teaspoon vanilla
1/2 teaspoon baking soda

Heat oven to 250 degrees. Combine cereal and pecans in a 9x13 inch baking pan. Set aside. Combine corn syrup, brown sugar and margarine in a 2 cup bowl. Microwave on high 1 1/2 minutes, stir and turn bowl. Microwave on high about 1 minute or until boiling. Stir in vanilla and soda. Pour over cereal mixture, stirring well to coat evenly. Bake in oven one hour, stirring every 20 minutes. Spread on baking sheet to cool.

This is great munching!

Crazy Cocoa Crisps

24 ounces white almond bark
2 1/4 cups Cocoa Krispies
2 cups dry roasted peanuts

Place almond bark in double boiler; heat, while stirring, until almond bark is melted. Stir in cereal and peanuts. Drop by teaspoon on cookie sheet. Store in airtight container.

Hot and Sweet Mustard

2 cups Coleman's dry mustard
2 cups white vinegar
4 eggs, beaten
2 cups sugar
1/8 teaspoon salt

Soak dry mustard in vinegar overnight. Beat eggs, sugar and salt together; then add to vinegar mustard mixture. In top of double boiler, cook over low heat for approximately 15 minutes, stirring constantly. Mixture will resemble a custard consistency. Pour immediately into jars and seal. Store in refrigerator.

This is a wonderful mustard to serve with ham or pork and especially good on ham sandwiches!

CHRISTMAS MORNING PRESERVES

A Very Special Treat

2 cups dried apricots
2 2/3 cups water
2 cups chunk pineapple and juice, undrained
2 1/2 cups sugar
3 tablespoons lemon juice
1 (6 ounce) bottle red maraschino cherries
1 (6 ounce) bottle green maraschino cherries

Wash apricots and simmer in water (just cover the apricots) for 30 minutes. Add pineapple, pineapple juice, sugar and lemon juice. Cook slowly, stirring often, until thick and clear — about 40 minutes. Just before it is done, use your potato masher to "smash" it up just a little. Drain and halve cherries and add to mixture. Heat again; then pour into hot sterilized jars and seal. Process in boiling water bath for 20 minutes. Or you can just keep in the refrigerator and give away each jar to a friend. They will be delighted with this gift!

This is a delicacy!

WINE JELLY

2 cups white wine
1/2 cup water
1/2 cup lime juice
1 box Sure Jell
4 1/4 cups sugar

In a large saucepan (the jelly needs room to bubble up while cooking), combine the wine, water and lime juice. Bring to a boiling point and stir in the Sure Jell. Add the sugar and bring to a boiling point. Boil for 1 minute. Skim foam off the jelly and pour into jelly jars. Seal with paraffin.

Great served with pork!

Can be served as an appetizer by putting a little cream cheese on a cracker and then top with a dab of the wine jelly!

SPICED PECANS

2 cups sugar
1/2 cup water
2 teaspoons cinnamon
1/4 teaspoon salt
1 teaspoon ground nutmeg
1/2 teaspoon ground cloves
4 cups pecan halves

Combine all ingredients except pecans in deep dish. Mix well and cover with waxed paper. Microwave on high for 4 minutes. Stir. Microwave another 4 minutes. Add pecans; quickly mixing well. Spread out on waxed paper to cool. Break apart and store in covered container.

These will disappear! My friend made these for everybody in the bridge club — now we expect 'em every Christmas.

ORANGE PECANS

1 1/2 cups sugar
1/2 cup frozen orange juice concentrate
4 cups pecan halves

Cook sugar and orange juice concentrate until it is very bubbly and forms a soft ball in a cup of water. Pour in pecans and stir vigorously. Pour out on a sheet of waxed paper and spread pecans out. Cool. Break up into single halves. And enjoy!

MAPLE CINNAMON PECANS

1 egg white
1/2 teaspoon cold water
1/2 teaspoon maple flavoring
2 cups pecan halves
2/3 cup sugar
1/4 teaspoon salt
1/2 teaspoon cinnamon

Beat egg white, water and maple flavoring until frothy, but not stiff. Add pecans and stir gently until pecans are well coated. Add sugar, salt and cinnamon. Mix well. Place on a large pan (or cookie sheet) with sides. Bake at 225 degrees for 1 hour, stirring every 15 minutes.

CHRISTMAS POTPOURRI

3 fresh juniper sprigs
2 red rosebuds
2 bay leaves
Cinnamon chips
2 cloves
Assorted pine cones

10 drops rose oil
3 drops pine oil
6 drops cinnamon oil
1 tablespoon orrisroot
Dried rose blossoms

Combine the first 6 ingredients in a big ceramic bowl. In a separate dish, mix the oils with orrisroot. Stir this mixture into the first one and let mellow for a few weeks. Place the Potpourri in a dish and scatter the rose blossoms on top.

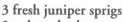

New Year's Day!

Something Green for Money — Black-Eyed Peas for Luck

CHEESY SPINACH

2 (10 ounce) packages frozen, chopped spinach
2 cups small curd cottage cheese
2 1/2 cups grated Cheddar cheese
4 eggs, beaten

3 tablespoons flour
1/2 stick margarine, melted
1/4 teaspoon garlic salt
1/4 teaspoon lemon pepper
1/4 teaspoon celery salt
1 teaspoon minced onion

Defrost spinach and squeeze out all water. Mix spinach with remaining ingredients and place in a 9x13 inch greased casserole. Bake at 325 degrees for 1 hour. Serves 10.

BLACK-EYED PEA SALAD

2 (16 ounce) cans Jalapeno black-eyed peas, drained
1 ripe avocado, peeled and chopped
1/2 purple onion, chopped
1 cup chopped celery
1 bell pepper, chopped

Dressing:
1/3 cup oil
1/3 cup white vinegar
3 tablespoons sugar
1/4 teaspoon garlic powder
1/2 teaspoon salt

In a large bowl, mix all salad ingredients together. Mix dressing ingredients together. Add dressing to vegetables and toss. Refrigerate. Serves 10.

INDEX

BCJ Publications
1901 South Shore Drive
Bonham, Texas 75418
903/583-8898

Please send ____ copy(ies) of

Holiday Treats   @ $ 7.95 each _____
                 Postage and Handling   @ $ 2.50 each _____
                 Texas residents add sales tax @ $ .43 each _____

Please send ____ copy(ies) of

Leaving Home   @ $ 12.95 each _____
                 Postage and Handling   @ $ 3.00 each _____
                 Texas residents add sales tax @ $ .97 each _____

Please send ____ copy(ies) of

A Little Taste of Texas   @ $ 6.95 each _____
                 Postage and Handling   @ $ 1.75 each _____
                 Texas residents add sales tax @ $ .52 each _____

Please send ____ copy(ies) of

A Little Taste of Texas II   @ $ 6.95 each _____
                 Postage and Handling   @ $ 1.75 each _____
                 Texas residents add sales tax @ $ .52 each _____

Please send ____ copy(ies) of

Southwest Sizzler   @ $ 6.95 each _____
                 Postage and Handling   @ $ 1.75 each _____
                 Texas residents add sales tax @ $ .52 each _____

Name _____

Address _____

City _____ State _____ Zip _____

Telephone _____

Charge to: ❑ Mastercard   ❑ Visa

Card # _____ Expiration Date _____

Name on Card (Please Print) _____

Signature _____